어머니
보고싶어

매
가고파
모
고양가
계고
다

DICTEE

Theresa Hak Kyung Cha

UNIVERSITY OF CALIFORNIA PRESS
Berkeley · Los Angeles · London

Library of Congress Cataloging-in-Publication Data

Cha, Theresa Hak Kyung.
    Dictee / Theresa Hak Kyung Cha.—1st California paperback ed.
      p. cm.
    Portions of text in English and French.
    Includes bibliographical references.
    ISBN 978-0-520-26129-7 (pbk. alk. : paper)
      1. Women—Poetry.   2. Loss (Psychology)—Poetry.
  3. Suffering—Poetry.   4. Exiles—Poetry. I. Title.

    PS3553.H13   D5   2001
    811'.54—dc21   2001027342

Originally published in 1982 by Tanam Press.

First Third Woman Press printing 1995.

First California paperback edition 2001.

Second paperback printing 2009.

Printed in the United States of America

19   18   17

13   12   11   10 9 8 7

The paper used in this publication meets the minimum requirements
of ANSI/NISO Z39.48-1992 (R 1997) (*Permanence of Paper*). ∞

TO MY MOTHER TO MY FATHER

May I write words more naked than flesh,
stronger than bone, more resilient than
sinew, sensitive than nerve.

Sappho

CLIO	HISTORY
CALLIOPE	EPIC POETRY
URANIA	ASTRONOMY
MELPOMENE	TRAGEDY
ERATO	LOVE POETRY
ELITERE	LYRIC POETRY
THALIA	COMEDY
TERPSICHORE	CHORAL DANCE
POLYMNIA	SACRED POETRY

Aller à la ligne   C'était le premier jour   point
Elle venait de loin   point   ce soir au dîner   virgule
les familles demanderaient   virgule   ouvre les guillemets   Ça c'est bien passé le premier jour   point
d'interrogation   ferme les guillemets   au moins
virgule   dire le moins possible   virgule   la réponse
serait   virgule   ouvre les guillemets   Il n'y a q'une
chose   point   ferme les guillemets   ouvre les guillemets   Il y a quelqu'une   point   loin   point   ferme
les guillemets

Open paragraph   It was the first day   period
She had come from a far   period   tonight at dinner
comma   the families would ask   comma   open
quotation marks   How was the first day   interrogation mark   close quotation marks   at least to say
the least of it possible   comma   the answer would be
open quotation marks   there is but one thing   period
There is someone   period   From   a far   period
close quotation marks

1

→ The book <u>Haunted</u>.

DISEUSE

She mimicks the speaking. That might resemble speech. (Anything at all.) Bared noise, groan, bits torn from words. Since she hesitates to measure the accuracy, she resorts to mimicking gestures with the mouth. The entire lower lip would lift upwards then sink back to its original place. She would then gather both lips and protrude them in a pout taking in the breath that might utter some thing. (One thing. Just one.) But the breath falls away. With a slight tilting of her head backwards, she would gather the strength in her shoulders and remain in this position.

It murmurs inside. It murmurs. Inside is the pain of speech the pain to say. Larger still. Greater than is the pain not to say. To not say. Says nothing against the pain to speak. It festers inside. The wound, liquid, dust. Must break. Must void.

From the back of her neck she releases her shoulders free. She swallows once more. (Once more. One more time would do.) In preparation. It augments. To such a pitch. Endless drone, refueling itself. Autonomous. Self-generating. Swallows with last efforts last wills against the pain that wishes it to speak.

She allows others. In place of her. Admits others to make full. Make swarm. All barren cavities to make swollen. The others each occupying her. Tumorous

3

layers, expel all excesses until in all cavities she is flesh.

She allows herself caught in their threading, anonymously in their thick motion in the weight of their utterance. When the amplification stops there might be an echo. She might make the attempt then. The echo part. At the pause. When the pause has already soon begun and has rested there still. She waits inside the pause. Inside her. Now. This very moment. Now. She takes rapidly the air, in gulfs, in preparation for the distances to come. The pause ends. The voice wraps another layer. Thicker now even. From the waiting. The wait from pain to say. To not to. Say.

She would take on their punctuation. She waits to service this. Theirs. Punctuation. She would become, herself, demarcations. Absorb it. Spill it. Seize upon the punctuation. Last air. Give her. Her. The relay. Voice. Assign. Hand it. Deliver it. Deliver.

She relays the others. Recitation. Evocation. Offering. Provocation. The begging. Before her. Before them.

Now the weight begins from the uppermost back of her head, pressing downward. It stretches evenly, the entire skull expanding tightly all sides toward the front of her head. She gasps from its pressure, its contracting motion.

Inside her voids. It does not contain further. Rising from the empty below, pebble lumps of gas. Moisture. Begin to flood her. Dissolving her. Slow, slowed to deliberation. Slow and thick.

The above traces from her head moving downward closing her eyes, in the same motion, slower parting her mouth open together with her jaw and throat which the above falls falling just to the end not stopping there but turning her inside out in the same motion, shifting complete the whole weight to elevate upward.

Begins imperceptibly, near-perceptible. (Just once. Just one time and it will take.) She takes. She takes the pause. Slowly. From the thick. The thickness. From weighted motion upwards. Slowed. To deliberation even when it passed upward through her mouth again. The delivery. She takes it. Slow. The invoking. All the time now. All the time there is. Always. And all times. The pause. Uttering. Hers now. Hers bare. The utter.

O Muse, tell me the story
Of all these things, O Goddess, daughter of Zeus
Beginning wherever you wish, tell even us.

Ecrivez en francais:
1. If you like this better, tell me so at once.
2. The general remained only a little while in this place.
3. If you did not speak so quickly, they would understand you better.
4. The leaves have not fallen yet nor will they fall for some days.
5. It will fit you pretty well.
6. The people of this country are less happy than the people of yours.
7. Come back on the fifteenth of next month, no sooner and no later.
8. I met him downstairs by chance.
9. Be industrious: the more one works, the better one succeeds.
10. The harder the task, the more honorable the labor.
11. The more a man praises himself, the less inclined are others to praise him.
12. Go away more quietly next time.

Traduire en francais:
1. I want you to speak.
2. I wanted him to speak.
3. I shall want you to speak.
4. Are you afraid he will speak?
5. Were you afraid they would speak?
6. It will be better for him to speak to us.
7. Was it necessary for you to write?
8. Wait till I write.

9. Why didn't you wait so that I could write you?

Complétez les phrases suivantes:
1. Le lac est (geler) ce matin.
2. Je (se lever) quand ma mère m'appeler.
3. Elle (essuyer) la table avec une éponge.
4. Il (mener) son enfant à l'ecole.
5. Au marché on (acheter) des oeufs, de la viande et des legumes.
6. Il (jeter) les coquilles des noix qu'il (manger).
7. Ils (se promener) tous les soirs dans le rue.
8. Elle (préférer) le chapeau vert.
9. Je (espérer) que vous m' (appeler) de bonne heure.
10. Ils (envoyer) des cadeaux à leurs amis.

Tell me the story
Of all these things.
Beginning wherever you wish, tell even us.

Black ash from the Palm Hosannah. Ash. Kneel down on the marble the cold beneath rising through the bent knees. Close eyes and as the lids flutter, push out the tongue.

The Host Wafer (His Body. His Blood.) His. Dissolving in the mouth to the liquid tongue saliva (Wine to Blood. Bread to Flesh.) His. Open the eyes to the women kneeling on the left side. The right side. Only visible on their bleached countenances are the unevenly lit circles of rouge and their elongated tongues. In waiting. To receive. Him.

Waiting. Nearing, nearer and nearer to the altar of God. Infusion of the surplus perfumes, bee's wax, incense, flowers.

Place back the tongue. Now to the forehead, between the two brows or just above. Hands folded fingers laced to expel all extraneous space. One gesture. Solid. For Him.

By then he is again at the other end. He the one who deciphers he the one who invokes in the Name. He the one who becomes He. Man-God. Places blessed leaves blessed ashes from the blessed palms in the left hand. Black dot of ash on the forehead. Through Hosannah Hosannah in the Highest. Through the Mea Culpa Mea Culpa through my most grievous sin. Crucifixion to follow. Of Him. Of His son.

Stand not too quickly the stations looking down at the red of the carpet hand placed on triangle white fake lace scarf not to slip fall from the head, the head of hair the sin covered. The nails of the shoes snag on the carpet down the aisle to the water bowl the finger reach to make the cross from the same forehead side by side not to erase the dark ash to the chest once to the left shoulder once then to the right in the Name of the Three in One, the mystery of all Three being One. At the same time. Nine steps down from the main gate is dusk now, evening, nightfall.

Translate into French:
1. Today would be the Feast day of the Immaculate Conception. She would have been voted to crown the Blessed Virgin. She herself would be sinless would be pure would be chaste in her heart. She would be silent. Often. Most of the time. Most often than not. Far too often.
2. "O my God, I am heartily sorry for having offended Thee, and I detest all my sins because of Thy just punishments, but most of all, because they offend Thee my God, who art all good and deserving of all my love. I firmly resolve the help of Thy grace to sin no more and to avoid the near occasion of sin, Amen."
3. Near Occasion
4. France was formerly divided into thirty-two provinces, such as Brittany, Provence, Franche-Comte, etc., but since the Revolution of seventeen eighty-nine, it is divided into eighty-six departments. The names given to the departments come almost all from the rivers that traverse them, such as the Loire, the Seine, etc.; some are borrowed from the names of the mountains, and a small

number from the situation, such as the Department of the North, or from the nature of the soil. Each department is administered by a prefect. Paris is not only the capital of France, it is the capital of the world. Do you know that there are about ten thousand Americans in Paris, who would quit to go to heaven?

5. She call she believe she calling to she has calling because there no response she believe she calling and the other end must hear. The other end must see the other end feel
she accept pages sent care of never to be seen never to be read never to be known if name if name be known if name only seen heard spoken read cannot be never she hide all essential words words link subject verb she writes hidden the essential words must be pretended invented she try on different images essential invisible

6. We left London at half past seven and arrived at Dover after a journey of two hours. At ten o'clock the boat left the harbour. The trip across the channel took only an hour and a half. The sea was calm, we did not feel the slightest of motion. We made a stop of an hour at Calais, where we had luncheon. It was rather dear but well served. At six o'clock in the evening we were in Paris. The entire trip was only a matter of a little more than ten hours and an expenditure of fifty francs.

7. Forget and would be forgotten close eyes and would be forgotten not say and they are forgotten not admit and they are forgotten like sins say

15

them they are forgiven forgotten and they are forgotten
8. In the name of the Father, and of the Son, and the
Holy Spirit, Amen. Bless me father, for I have
sinned, my last confession was... I can't remember. Name how many; one. two. three.
weeks months years.
Name all the sins.
Name all the mortal sins if any, how many.
Name all the venial sins, how many.
Get the penance.
Say thank you Father.   France
Say all the penance.   ⁀ Athump.
9. The young poet who composed the Marseillaise
was called Rouget de Lisle. He wrote it when he
was in Strassburg in March or April, seventeen
ninety-two. He spent a whole night composing
this beautiful song; however, he wrote nothing
before the next morning. After writing what he
had composed, he went to the house of his friend
Dietrich to show it to him. He sang his new song
before his friends. The mayor's wife accompanied
him at the piano. Everyone applauded. Soon it
was sung everywhere in France.

"Bless me father, for I have sinned. My last confession was... I can't remember when... These are my
sins."

*I am making up the sins. For the guarantee of ab-
solution. In the beginning again, at zero. Before
Heaven even. Before the Fall. All previous*

16

wrongs erased. *Reduced to spotless. Pure. When I receive God, all pure. Totally. For the Dwelling of God Housed in my body and soul must be clean. Free of sin. Any sin. Mortal sin. The greater the sin, greater the forgiveness, greater the Glory of God in His forgiveness. I have none. Venial sin. Small sins. Hardly worth the mention. Sins, all the same. Thoughts even. No matter how invisible. Everything is visible to God. Thought as visible as word as act.*

Act of Contrition. I am making the confession. To make words. To make a speech in such tongues.

Q: WHO MADE THEE?

A: *God made me.*

To conspire in God's Tongue.

Q: WHERE IS GOD?

A: *God is everywhere.*

Accomplice in His Texts, the fabrication in His Own Image, the pleasure the desire of giving Image to the word in the mind of the confessor.

Q: GOD WHO HAS MADE YOU IN HIS OWN LIKENESS.

A: *God who has made me in His own likeness. In His Own Image in His Own Resemblance, in His Own Copy, In His Own Counterfeit Present-ment, in His Duplicate, in His Own Reproduc-tion, in His Cast, in His Carbon, His Image and His Mirror. Pleasure in the image pleasure in the copy pleasure in the projection of likeness pleasure in the repetition. Acquiesce, to the cor-*

17

respondance. Acquiesce, to the messenger. Acquiesce, to and for the complot in the Hieratic tongue. Theirs. Into Their tongue, the counter-script, my confession in Theirs. Into Theirs. To scribe to make hear the words, to make sound the words, the words, the words made flesh.

First Friday. One hour before mass. Mass every First Friday. Dictée first. Every Friday. Before mass. Dictée before. Back in the study hall. It is time. Snaps once. One step right from the desk. Single file. Snaps twice. Follow single line. Move all the way to the right hand side of the wall. Single file. The sound instrument is made from two pieces of flat box-shaped wood, with a hinge at the center. It rests inside the palm and is snapped with a defined closing of the thumb. Framed inside is an image of the Holy Virgin Mary robed in blue with white drape or white robe with a blue drape over her head, her eyes towards Heaven, two hands to Heaven, shrouded in clouds, the invisible feet. Framed inside next to her is the sacred heart of Jesus, a pierced heart enflamed single threaded thorn across above emanating silver light. Image of Jesus Christ pointing his left index finger to chest wounded mark on right hand reaching reaching perhaps ever so gently.
Single file silence gliding steps one at a time
the organ has started already
Les enfants de Mon Sacré Coeur. (All capital letters)
The organ plays over again
Vous l'avez dit Votre Promesse...nos espoir notre

18

bonheure (or was it votre) dans la tendresse... (or was it ma tendresse)
les enfants de Mon Sacre Coeur
over and over
the single file waits at the door of the chapel. The seniors first. The line divides in two. Waiting in two lines with space between. The singing has begun. The words are in the blue books in case you have forgotten them. The chosen ones to crown Mary the Immaculate Conception enter in the center. The white uniforms. The ribbon of satin, today, blue draped across from the right shoulder down to the left side of the waist. Banner. Of blue and white satin. The image of Mary seated. In the center. White lilies. One in the center to carry the banner. The eight others, 4 by 4 in single file behind the one with the banner. 9 in all. Each pew holds nine. One monitor to count the nine then to the next pew. The next verse. And then back to the first. Over and over. Until it begins. The novena of the Immaculate Conception.

NOVENA: NINE EACH. THE RECITATION OF PRAYER AND PRACTICING OF DEVOTIONS DURING A NINE DAY PERIOD

And it begins.

From A Far
What nationality
or what kindred and relation
what blood relation
what blood ties of blood
what ancestry
what race generation
what house clan tribe stock strain
what lineage extraction
what breed sect gender denomination caste
what stray ejection misplaced
Tertium Quid neither one thing nor the other
Tombe des nues de naturalized
what transplant to dispel upon

IN NOMINE

LE NOM

NOMINE

CLIO   HISTORY

YU GUAN SOON

BIRTH: By Lunar Calendar, 15, March 1903
DEATH: 12, October, 1920. 8:20 A.M.

She is born of one mother and one father.

She makes complete her duration. As others have made complete theirs: rendered incessant, obsessive myth, rendered immortal their acts without the leisure to examine whether the parts false the parts real according to History's revision.

Truth embraces with it all other abstentions other than itself. Outside Time. Outside Space. Parallels other durations, oblivious to the deliberate brilliance of its own time, mortal, deliberate marking. Oblivious to itself. But to sing. To sing to. Very softly.

She calls the name Jeanne d'Arc three times.
She calls the name Ahn Joong Kun five times.

There is no people without a nation, no people without ancestry. There are other nations no matter how small their land, who have their independence. But our country, even with 5,000 years of history, has lost it to the Japanese.

"Japan at once created an assembly, in the name of the King, for the 'discussion of everything, great and small, that happened within the realm.' This assembly at first met daily, and afterwards at longer intervals. There were soon no less than fifty Japanese advisers at work in Seoul. They were men of little experience and less responsibility, and they apparently thought that they were going to transform the land between the rising and setting of the sun. They produced endless ordinances, and scarce a day went by save that a number of new regulations were issued, some trivial, some striking at the oldest and most cherished institutions in the country. The Government was changed from an absolute monarchy to one where the king governed only by the advice of the Ministers. The power of direct address to the throne was denied to anyone under the rank of Governor. One ordinance created a constitution, and the next dealt with the status of the ladies of the royal seraglio. At one hour a proclamation went forth that all men were to cut their hair, and the wearied runners on their return were again dispatched in hot haste with an edict altering the official language. Nothing was too small, nothing too great, and nothing too contradictory for these constitution-mongers. Their doings were the laugh and the amazement of every foreigner in the place.

"Acting on the Japanese love of order and of defined rank, exact titles of honour were provided for the wives of officials. These were divided into nine grades: 'Pure and Reverent Lady,' 'Pure Lady,' 'Chaste Lady,' 'Chaste Dame,' 'Worthy Dame,' 'Courteous Dame,' 'Just Dame,' 'Peaceful Dame,' and 'Upright Dame.' At the same time the King's concubines were equally divided, but here eight divisions were sufficient: 'Mistress,' 'Noble Lady,' 'Resplendent Exemplar,' 'Chaste Exemplar,' 'Resplendent Demeanor,' 'Chaste Demeanor,' 'Resplendent Beauty,' and 'Chaste Beauty.' The Japanese advisers instituted a number of sumptuary laws that stirred the country to its depths, relating to the length of pipes, style of dress, and the attiring of the hair of the people. Pipes were to be short, in place of the long bamboo churchwarden beloved by the Koreans.

Sleeves were to be clipped. The top-knot, worn by all Korean men, was at once to be cut off. Soldiers at the city gates proceeded to enforce this last regulation rigorously."

Guan Soon is the only daughter born of four children to her patriot father and mother. From an early age her actions are marked exceptional. History records the biography of her short and intensely-lived existence. Actions prescribed separate her path from the others. The identity of such a path is exchangeable with any other heroine in history, their names, dates, actions which require not definition in their devotion to generosity and self-sacrifice.

In Guan Soon's 16th year, 1919, the conspiracy by the Japanese to overthrow the Korean Government is achieved with the assassination of the ruling Queen Min and her royal family. In the aftermath of this incident, Guan Soon forms a resistant group with fellow students and actively begins her revolutionary work. There is already a nationally organized movement, who do not accept her seriousness, her place as a young woman, and they attempt to dissuade her. She is not discouraged and demonstrates to them her conviction and dedication in the cause. She is appointed messenger and she travels on foot to 40 towns, organizing the nation's mass demonstration to be held on March 1, 1919. This date marks the turning point, it is the largest collective outcry against the Japanese occupation of the Korean people who willingly gave their lives for independence.

The only daughter of four children she makes complete her life as others have made complete. Her mother her father her brothers.

" 'I saw four places where engagements had been fought. At one place it had been a drawn battle, the Japanese retiring with five killed. The other three were Japanese victories, owing to the long range of their rifles and their superior ammunition; and only one of their victories was obtained without casualties to themselves. I saw enough to realise that it was no picnic for the Japanese.

" 'One is forced to ask who is in charge of these men who are nothing more than brigands. Their mode of warfare seems to be purposely designed to stir every honest man into a frenzy. Is this their object? If not, why do they practice so wicked, so mad a policy? Let the authorities either police the whole disaffected districts effectually and properly, or else confess their incapacity for controlling Korea.' "

SUPPRESSION OF FOREIGN CRITICISM
September 26, 1907

"We are informed that a bad fight took place about eight miles from Su-won on Sunday, September 12th. Thirty volunteers were surrounded by Japanese troops, and although no resistance was offered, they were shot down in the most cold-blooded fashion. This not being quite enough to satisfy the conquerors, two other volunteers who had been captured were brought out and were decapitated by one of the officers. We may mention that this news does not come from native sources; it comes from European."

The "enemy." One's enemy. Enemy nation. Entire nation against the other entire nation. One people exulting the suffering institutionalized on another. The enemy becomes abstract. The relationship becomes abstract. The nation the enemy the name becomes larger than its own identity. Larger than its own measure. Larger than its own properties. Larger than its own signification. For *this* people. For the people who is their enemy. For the people who is their ruler's subject and their ruler's victory.

Japan has become the sign. The alphabet. The vocabulary. To *this* enemy people. The meaning is the instrument, memory that pricks the skin, stabs the flesh, the volume of blood, the physical substance blood as measure, that rests as record, as document. Of *this* enemy people.

To the other nations who are not witnesses, who are not subject to the same oppressions, they cannot know. Unfathomable the words, the terminology: enemy, atrocities, conquest, betrayal, invasion, desstruction. They exist only in the larger perception of History's recording, that affirmed, admittedly and unmistakably, one enemy nation has disregarded the humanity of another. Not physical enough. Not to the very flesh and bone, to the core, to the mark, to the point where it is necessary to intervene, even if to invent anew, expressions, for *this* experience, for this *outcome*, that does not cease to continue.

To the others, these accounts are about (one more) distant land, like (any other) distant land, without any discernable features in the narrative, (all the same) distant like any other.

This document is transmitted through, by the same means, the same channel without distinction the content is delivered in the same style: the word. The image. To appeal to the masses to congeal the information to make bland, mundane, no longer able to transcend their own conspirator method, no matter how alluring their presentation. The response is precoded to perform predictably however passively possible. Neutralized to achieve the no-response, to make absorb, to submit to the uni-directional correspondance.

Why resurrect it all now. From the Past. History, the old wound. The past emotions all over again. To confess to relive the same folly. To name it now so as not to repeat history in oblivion. To extract each fragment by each fragment from the word from the image another word another image the reply that will not repeat history in oblivion.

PETITION FROM THE KOREANS OF HAWAII TO PRESIDENT ROOSEVELT

Honolulu, T.H.
July 12, 1905

To His Excellency,
The President of the United States

Your Excellency,—The undersigned have been authorised by the 8,000 Koreans now residing in the territory of Hawaii at a special mass meeting held in the city of Honolulu, on July 12, 1905, to present to your Excellency the following appeal:—

We, the Koreans of the Hawaiian Islands, voicing the sentiments of twelve millions of our countrymen, humbly lay before your Excellency the following facts:—

Soon after the commencement of the war between Russia and Japan, our Government made a treaty of alliance with Japan for offensive and defensive purposes. By virtue of this treaty the whole of Korea was opened to the Japanese, and both the Government and the people have been assisting the Japanese authorities in their military operations in and about Korea.

The contents of this treaty are undoubtedly known to your Excellency, therefore we need not embody them in this appeal. Suffice it to state, however, the object of the treaty was to preserve the independence of Korea and Japan and to protect Eastern Asia from Russia's aggression.

Korea, in return for Japan's friendship and protection against Russia, has rendered services to the Japanese by permitting them to use the country as a base of their military operations.

When this treaty was concluded, the Koreans fully expected that Japan would introduce reforms into the governmental administration along the line of the modern civilization of Europe and America, and that she would advise and counsel our people in a friendly manner, but to our disappointment and regret the Japanese Government has not done a single thing in the way of improving the condition of the Korean people. On the contrary, she turned loose several thousand rough and disorderly men of her nationals in Korea, who are treating the inoffensive Koreans in a most outrageous manner. The Koreans are by nature not a quarrelsome or aggressive people, but deeply resent the high-handed action of the Japanese towards them. We can scarcely believe that the Japanese Government approves the outrages committed by its people in Korea, but it has done nothing to prevent this state of affairs. They have been, during the last eighteen months, forcibly obtaining all the special privileges and concessions from our Government, so that to-day they practically own everything that is worth having in Korea.

We, the common people of Korea, have lost confidence in the promises Japan made at the time of concluding the treaty of alliance, and we doubt seriously the good intentions which she professes to have towards our people. For geographical, racial, and commercial reasons we want to be friendly to Japan, and we are even willing to have her as our guide and example in the matters of internal reforms and education, but the continuous policy of self-exploitation at the expense of the Koreans has shaken our confidence in her, and we are now afraid that she will not keep her promise of preserving our independence as a nation, nor assisting us in reforming internal administration. In other words, her policy in Korea seems to be exactly the same as that of Russia prior to the war.

The United States has many interests in our country. The industrial, commercial, and religious enterprises under American management, have attained such proportions that we believe the Government and people of the Unites States ought to know the true conditions of Korea and the result of the Japanese becoming paramount in our country. We know that the people of America love fair play and advocate justice towards all men. We also know that your Excellency is the ardent exponent of a square deal between individuals as well as nations, therefore we come to you with this memorial with the hope that Your Excellency may help our country at this critical period of our national life.

We fully appreciate the fact that during the conference between the Russian and Japanese peace envoys, Your Excellency may not care to make any suggestion to either party as to the conditions of their settlement, but we earnestly hope that Your Excellency will see to it that Korea may preserve her autonomous Government and that other Powers shall not oppress or maltreat our people. The clause in the treaty between the United States and Korea gives us a claim upon the United States for assistance, and this is the time when we need it most.

Very respectfully, Your obedient servants,
(*Sgd.*) P.K. Yoon
Syngman Rhee

March 1, 1919. Everyone knows to carry inside themselves, the national flag. Everyone knows equally the punishment that follows this gesture. The march begins, the flags are taken out, made visible, waved, every individual crying out the independence the freedom to the people of this nation. Knowing equally the punishment. Her parents leading the procession fell. Her brothers. Countless others were fired at and stabbed indiscriminately by the enemy soldiers. Guan Soon is arrested as a leader of the revolution, with punishment deserving of such a rank. She is stabbed in the chest, and subjected to questioning to which she reveals no names. She is given seven years prison sentence to which her reply is that the nation itself is imprisoned. Child revolutionary child patriot woman soldier deliverer of nation. The eternity of one act. Is the completion of one existence. One martyrdom. For the history of one nation. Of one people.

Some will not know age. Some not age. Time stops. Time will stop for some. For them especially. Eternal time. No age. Time fixes for some. Their image, the memory of them is not given to deterioration, unlike the captured image that extracts from the soul precisely by reproducing, multiplying itself. Their countenance evokes not the hallowed beauty, beauty from seasonal decay, evokes not the inevitable, not death, but the dy-ing.

Face to face with the memory, it misses. It's missing. Still. What of time. Does not move. Remains there.

Misses nothing. Time, that is. All else. All things else. All other, subject to time. Must answer to time, except. Still born. Aborted. Barely. Infant. Seed, germ, sprout, less even. Dormant. Stagnant. Missing.

The decapitated forms. Worn. Marred, recording a past, of previous forms. The present form face to face reveals the missing, the absent. Would-be-said remnant, memory. But the remnant is the whole.

The memory is the entire. The longing in the face of the lost. Maintains the missing. Fixed between the wax and wane indefinite not a sign of progress. All else age, in time. Except. Some are without.

Some will not know age.

stop for some. For them

~~At deterioration.~~ Time fi

Their image, ~~this me~~ the memo

~~captured~~ the hallowed beauty that

Standing before hallowed be

~~loss, the absence, the pre~~

missing ~~sketche~~ left to the

Their countenance evokes

the inevitable ∧ the dy-ing.

not death, but

~~Standing before hallowed bec~~

Standing face to face with

missing. still. what of time

Misses nothing. Time, that is

all ~~off~~ things other. Subject

Time dictates all else, exa

age. Time stops. Time will

cially. Eternal time. No age.

or some. ~~In their view~~

em. ~~On their countenance~~

~~of~~ evidence

~~only~~

The ~~only~~ beauty, ~~because of the~~ ~~that connects~~

, only because

it ~~presents~~ the loss, the

exposes

maginary.

the   Evokes not the

~~the~~ beauty, ~~attaching~~ the decay

hallowed beauty from the

~~only because~~

~~The beauty, that is~~

~~now~~ memory of. It misses. it's

not more. remains there.

ll else. all things else.

re. Must answer to time.

e.

misses. All installed in time,

CALLIOPE   EPIC POETRY

Cha mother
Huo Hyung Soon.

Mother, you are eighteen years old. You were born in Yong Jung, Manchuria and this is where you now live. You are not Chinese. You are Korean. But your family moved here to escape the Japanese occupation. China is large. Larger than large. You tell me that the hearts of the people are measured by the size of the land. As large and as silent. You live in a village where the other Koreans live. Same as you. Refugees. Immigrants. Exiles. Farther away from the land that is not your own. Not your own any longer.

You did not want to see. You cannot see anymore. What they do. To the land and to the people. As long as the land is not your own. Until it will be again. Your father left and your mother left as the others. You suffer the knowledge of having to leave. Of having left. But your MAH-UHM, spirit has not left. Never shall have and never shall will. Not now. Not even now. It is burned into your ever-present memory. Memory less. Because it is not in the past. It cannot be. Not in the least of all pasts. It burns. Fire alight enflame.

Mother, you are a child still. At eighteen. More of a child since you are always ill. They have sheltered you from life. Still, you speak the tongue the mandatory language like the others. It is not your own. Even if it is not you know you must. You are Bilingual. You are Tri-lingual. The tongue that is forbidden is your own mother tongue. You speak in the dark. In the secret. The one that is yours. Your own. You speak very softly, you speak in a whisper. In the dark, in secret. Mother tongue is your refuge. It is being home. Being who you are. Truly. To speak makes you sad. Yearning. To utter each word is a privilege you risk by death. Not only for you but for all. All of you who are one, who by law tongue tied forbidden of tongue. You carry at center the mark of the red above and the mark of blue below, heaven and earth, tai-geuk; t'ai-chi. It is the mark. The mark of belonging. Mark of cause. Mark of retreival. By birth. By death. By blood. You carry the mark in your chest, in your MAH-UHM, in your MAH-UHM, in your spirit-heart.

You sing.

Standing in a shadow, Bong Sun flower
Your form is destitute
Long and long inside the summer day
When beautifully flowers bloom
The lovely young virgins will
Have played in your honor.

In truth this would be the anthem. The national song forbidden to be sung. Birth less. And orphan. They take from you your tongue. They take from you the choral hymn. But you say not for long not for always. Not forever. You wait. You know how. You know how to wait. Inside MAH-UHM fire alight enflame.

From the Misere to Gloria to Magnificat and
Sanctus. To the Antiphonal song. Because
surely. Soon. The answer would come. The
response. Like echo. After the oblations. The
offering. The sacrifice, the votive, the devotions,

46

the novenas, the matins, the lauds, the vespers,
the vigils, the evensong, the nightsong, the atten-
dance, the adoration, the veneration, the honor,
the invocations, the supplications, the petitions,
the recitations, the vows, the immolations.
Surely, all these and more. Ceaseless. Again.
Over and over.

You know to wait. Wait in the Misere. Wait in the
Gloria. Wait in the Magnificat. Wait in the Sanctus.
For the Antiphonal song. Antiphonal hymn. The
choral answer. In the ebb and tide of echo.

They have not forbidden sight to your eyes. You
see. You are made to see. You see and you know. For
yourself. The eyes have not been condemned. You
see inspite of. Your sight. Let that be a lesson to you.
You see farther. Farther and farther. Beyond what
you are made to see and made to see only. You pass
the mark, even though you say nothing. Everyone
who has seen, sees farther. Even farther than allowed. And you wait. You keep silent. You bide
time. Time. Single stone laid indicating the day from
sunrise to sundown. Filling up times belly. Stone by
stone. Three hundred sixty five days multiplied thirty
six years. Some have been born into it. And some
would die into it.

The days before the reclamation. Your father.
Your mother. Dying while uttering the words. Their
only regret. Not having seen with their very eyes, the
overthrow. The repelling. The expulsion of the people who have taken you by force. Not to have wit-
nessed the purging by sulphur and fire. Of the house.
Of the nation.

You write. You write you speak voices hidden masked you plant words to the moon you send word through the wind. Through the passing of seasons. By sky and by water the words are given birth given discretion. From one mouth to another, from one reading to the next the words are realized in their full meaning. The wind. The dawn or dusk the clay earth and traveling birds south bound birds are mouth pieces wear the ghost veil for the seed of message. Correspondence. To scatter the words.

Mother you are eighteen. It is 1940. You have just graduated from a teacher's college. You are going to your first teaching post in a small village in the country. Your are required by the government of Manchuria to teach for three years in an assigned post, to repay the loan they provided for you to attend the teacher's school. You are hardly an adult. You have never left your mother's, father's home. You who are born the youngest of four children. Always ailing. You have been sheltered from the harshness of daily life. Always the youngest of the family, the child.

You traveled to this village on the train with your father. You are dressed in western clothes. At the station the villagers innocently stare at you and some follow you, especially the children. It is Sunday.

You are the first woman teacher to come to this village in six years. A male teacher greets you, he addresses you in Japanese. Japan had already occupied Korea and is attempting the occupation of China. Even in the small village the signs of their

48

presence is felt by the Japanese language that is being spoken. The Japanese flag is hanging at the entry of the office. And below it, the educational message of the Meiji emperor framed in purple cloth. It is read at special functions by the principal of the school to all the students.

The teachers speak in Japanese to each other. You are Korean. All the teachers are Korean. You are assigned to teach the first grade. Fifty children to your class. They must speak their name in Korean as well as how they should be called in Japanese. You speak to them in Korean since they are too young yet to speak Japanese.

It is February. In Manchuria. In this village you are alone and your hardships are immense. You are timid and unaccustomed to the daily existence of these village people. Outside the room and board that you pay, you send the rest of your pay home. You cannot ask for more than millet and barley to eat. You take what is given to you. Always do. Always have. You. Your people.

You take the train home. Mother. . .you call her already, from the gate. Mother, you cannot wait. She leaves everything to greet you, she comes and takes you indoors and brings you food to eat. You are home now your mother your home. Mother inseparable from which is her identity, her presence. Longing to breathe the same air her hand no more a hand than instrument broken weathered no death takes them. No death will take them, Mother, I dream you just to be able to see you. Heaven falls nearer in

49

sleep. Mother, my first sound. The first utter. The first concept.

It is Sunday afternoon. You must return to the school. Your students are at the station waiting for you. They see you home and bring you food. It is May, it is still cold in Manchuria. You work Monday, Tuesday, Wednesday, and Thursday passes. On Friday morning you do not feel well. Fever and chill possess the body at the same time. You are standing in the sunlight against the tepid wall to warm yourself. You are giving in. To the fall to the lure behind you before you all around you beneath your skin the sharp air begins to blow the winds of the body, dark fires rising to battle for victory, the summoning the coaxing the irresistable draw replacing sleep dense with images condensing them without space in between. No drought to the extentions of spells, words, noise. Music equally out of proportion. You are yielding to them. They are too quick to arrive. You do not know them, never have seen them but they seek you, inhabit you whole, suspend you airless, spaceless. They force their speech upon you and direct your speech only to them.

You are going somewhere. You are somewhere. This stillness. You cannot imagine how. Still. So still all around. Such stillness. It is endless. Spacious without the need for verification of space. Nothing moves. So still. There is no struggle. Its own all its own. No where other. No time other conceivable. Total duration without need for verification of time.

You are moving inside. Inside the stillness. Its slowness makes almost imperceptible the movement. Pauses. Pauses hardly rest. New movement, ending only to extend into the next movement. Stops as elongation into the new movement. You say this is how Heaven should be. You say this is how it must be death. (Memoryless. Dreamless.) Afterwards. The thick the weight of stillness. You are moving accordingly never ahead of the movement never behind the movement you are carrying the weight from outside being the weight inside. You move. You are being moved. You are movement. Inseparably. Indefinably. Not isolatable terms. None. Nothing.

You come to a house. Enormous in size. There are women standing before the house dressed in costumes made of a strange and beautiful cloth. They are carried in a light breeze faintly lifting above ground as if their bodies wore wings. From the distance their movements are reduced to make almost clearer the movement.

To one side of the house you see a very wide flower bed. There is no end in sight. You pass along it when you come upon a very large hall where an orchestra is playing music. On the other side, some women draped in long silk cloths are dancing. They entrance you. Numb you. You watch in awe for what seems to be a very long time. Such calm, you cannot imagine an expression that would describe it. Curiosity pulls you further and you move towards what looks like a restaurant. There are people very well dressed in not our native costumes and not foreign costumes. You pass them and walk for a long time. From the opposite direction, three women are approaching you. Their strange beauty increases with their slow progression towards you. You notice that they each carry a large dish of food. You cannot identify its origin, but it captivates you completely.

Their spirit takes your own. You are immobilized they hold you to their sight and approach even nearer. They smile to you they say to you they have prepared this food especially for you. The first one stands facing you and asks you to eat from it. You shake your head in refusal inspite of its aroma and the beautiful arrangement.

> Then was Jesus led up of the Spirit into the wilderness to be tempted of the devil.
>
> 2 And when he had fasted forty days and forty nights, he was afterward ahungered.
>
> 3 And when the tempter came to him, he said, If thou be the Son of God, command that these stones be made bread.
>
> 4 But he answered and said, it is written, Man shall not live by bread alone, but by every word that proceedeth out of the mouth of God.

The second one offers you from her dish and you refuse again. You cannot speak you only shake your head in disagreement.

> 5 Then the devil taketh him up into the holy city, and setteth him on a pinnacle of the temple,
>
> 6 And saith unto him, If thou be the Son of God, cast thyself down: for it is written, He shall give his angels charge concerning thee: and in their hand they shall bear thee up, lest at any time thou dash thy foot against a stone.

7 Jesus said unto him It is written again, Thou shall not tempt the Lord thy God.

The third one says to you, "then you must eat from mine."

8 Again, the devil taketh him up into an exceeding high mountain, and showeth him all the kingdoms of the world, and the glory of them;

9 And saith unto him, All these things will I give thee, if thou wilt fall down and worship me.

10 Then saith Jesus unto him, Get thee hence, Satan: for it is written, Thou shalt worship the Lord thy God, and him only shalt thou serve.

11 Then the devil leaveth him, and behold, angels came and ministered unto him.

You cannot accept and the third one pushes you down and says, "If you do not eat, you must become a cripple!" You fall. You fall deep.

Your mother holds your hand and your father your right hand your fingers begin to curl you ask them to unfold them. You feel on your hands the warm tears from your mother and father. They say when one is about to die the fingers curl to a close. She has eaten nothing your father's voice saying how can she live. Upon hearing this you ask to eat. They say that the dying ask for food as a last wish. They give you to eat.

No more sentence to exile, Mother, no black crows to mourn you. Neither takes you neither will take you Heaven nor Hell they fall too near you let them fall to each other you come back you come back to your one mother to your one father.

I write. I write you. Daily. From here. If I am not writing, I am thinking about writing. I am composing. Recording movements. You are here I raise the voice. Particles bits of sound and noise gathered pick up lint, dust. They might scatter and become invisible. Speech morsels. Broken chips of stones. Not hollow not empty. They think that you are one and the same direction addressed. The vast ambiant sound hiss between the invisible line distance that this line connects the void and space surrounding entering and exiting.

They have not questioned. It is all the same to them. It follows directions. Not yet. They have not learned the route of instruction. To surpass overtake the hidden even beyond destination. Destination.

I have the documents. Documents, proof, evidence, photograph, signature. One day you raise the right hand and you are American. They give you an American Pass port. The United States of America. Somewhere someone has taken my identity and replaced it with their photograph. The other one. Their signature their seals. Their own image. And you learn the executive branch the legislative branch and the third. Justice. Judicial branch. It makes the difference. The rest is past.

You return and you are not one of them, they treat you with indifference. All the time you understand what they are saying. But the papers give you away. Every ten feet. They ask you identity. They comment upon your inability or ability to speak. Whether you are telling the truth or not about your nationality.

They say you look other than you say. As if you didn't know who you were. You say who you are but you begin to doubt. They search you. They, the anonymous variety of uniforms, each division, strata, classification, any set of miscellaneous properly uni formed. They have the right, no matter what rank, however low their function they have the authority. Their authority sewn into the stitches of their costume. Every ten feet they demand to know who and what you are, who is represented. The eyes gather towards the appropriate proof. Towards the face then again to the papers, when did you leave the country why did you leave this country why are you returning to the country.

You see the color the hue the same you see the shape the form the same you see the unchangeable and the unchanged the same you smell filtered edited through progress and westernization the same you see the numerals and innumerables bonding overlaid the same, speech, the same. You see the will, you see the breath, you see the out of breath and out of will but you still see the will. Will and will only espouse this land this sky this time this people. You are one same particle. You leave you come back to the shell left empty all this time. To claim to reclaim, the space. Into the mouth the wound the entry is reverse and back each organ artery gland pace element, implanted, housed skin upon skin, membrane, vessel, waters, dams, ducts, canals, bridges.

Composition of the body, taking into consideration from conception, the soil, seed, amount of light and water necessary, the geneology. Not a single word allowed to utter until the last station, they ask to check the baggage. You open your mouth half way. Near tears, nearly saying, I know you I know you, I have waited to see you for long this long. They check each article, question you on foreign articles, then dismiss you.

URANIA   ASTRONOMY

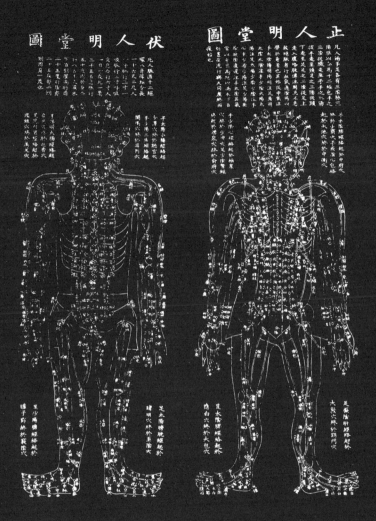

She takes my left arm, tells me to make a fist, then open. Make a fist then open again, make the vein appear through the skin blue-green-purple tint to the translucent surface. Pump them open and close. She takes the elastic band and ties it tightly around the left arm. She taps on the flesh presses against it her thumb. She removes the elastic to the right arm. Open and close the right hand, fist and palm. She takes the cotton and rubs alcohol lengthwise on the arm several times. The coolness disappears as the liquid begins to evaporate. She takes the needle with its empty body to the skin.
No sign of flow
Sample extract
Specimen type

> *Should it appear should it happen to appear all of a sudden, suddenly, begin to flow begin to collect begin to spill over flow flood should it happen to.*

Contents housed in membranes. Stain from within dispel in drops in spills. Contents of other recesses seep outward.

Too long. Enough already. One empty body waiting to contain. Conceived for a single purpose and for the purpose only. To contain. Made filled. Be full. She pulls out the needle and the skin lifts.

> *Should it happen that the near-black liquid ink draws the line from point mark gravity follow (inevitably, suddenly) in one line down the arm*

on the table in one long spill, exhale of a spill.

It takes her seconds less to break the needle off its body in attempt to collect the loss directly from the wound.

Stain begins to absorb the material spilled on.

She pushes hard the cotton square against the mark.

Stain begins to absorb the material spilled on.

Something of the ink that resembles the stain from the interior emptied onto emptied into emptied upon this boundary this surface. More. Others. When possible ever possible to puncture to scratch to imprint. Expel. Ne te cache pas. Révèle toi. Sang. Encre. Of its body's extention of its containment.

J'écoutais les cygnes.
Les cygnes dans la pluie. J'écoutais.
J'ai entendu des paroles vrai
ou pas vrai
impossible à dire.

Là. Des années après
Impossible de distinguer la Pluie.
Cygnes. Paroles souvenus. Déjà dit.
Vient de dire. Va dire.
Souvenu mal entendu. Pas certain.

La Pluie fait rêver de sons.
Des Pauses. Exhalation.
Des affirmations toutes les affirmations.

Peu à peu

Impossible de distinguer les paroles
Exhalées. Affirmées en exhalation
exclamées en inhalation
Ne plus distinguer la pluie des rêves
ou des souffles

La langue dedans. La bouche dedans
la gorge dedans
le poumon l'organe seul
Tout ensemble un. Une.

I heard the swans
in the rain I heard
I listened to the spoken true
or not true
not possible to say.

There. Years after
no more possible to distinguish the rain.
No more. Which was heard.
Swans. Speech. Memory. Already said.
Will just say. Having just said.
Remembered not quite heard. Not certain.
Heard, not at all.

Rain dreamed from sounds.
The pauses. Exhalation.
Affirmations. All the affirmations.

Little by little

Not possible to distinguish the speech
Exhaled. Affirmed in exhalation.
Exclaimed in inhalation.
To distinguish no more the rain from dreams
or from breaths.

Tongue inside the mouth inside
the throat inside
the lung organ alone. The only organ.
All assembled as one. Just one.

Là. Plus tard, peu certain, si c'était
la pluie, la parole, mémoire.
Mémoire d'un rêve.
Comment cela s'éteint. Comment l'etéindre.
Alors que cela
s'éteint.

Mordre la langue.
Avaler profondément. Plus profondément.
Avaler. Plus encore.
Jusqu'a ce qu'il n'y aurait plus. D'organe.
Plus d'organe.
Cris.

Peu à peu. Les virgules. Les points.
Les pauses.
Avant et après. Tous les avants.
Tous les après.
Phrases.
Paragraphs. Silencieux. A peu près
des pages et des pages
en mouvement
lignes après
lignes
vides à gauche vides à droite, vides de mots.
de silences.

J'écoutais les signes.
Les signes muets. Jamais pareils.
Absents.

There. Later, uncertain, if it was
the rain, the speech, memory.
Re membered from dream.
How it diminishes itself. How to Dim
inish itself. As
it dims.

To bite the tongue.
Swallow. Deep. Deeper.
Swallow. Again even more.
Just until there would be no more of organ.
Organ no more.
Cries.

Little at a time. The commas. The periods.
The pauses.
Before and after. Throughout. All advent.
All following.
Sentences.
Paragraphs. Silent. A little nearer. Nearer
Pages and pages
in movement
line after
line
void to the left void to the right, void the
words the silences.

I heard the signs. Remnants. Missing.
The mute signs. Never the same.
Absent.

Images seulement. Seules. Images.
Les signes dans la pluie, j'écoutais.
Les paroles ne sont que pluie devenues neige.
Vrai ou pas vrai.
impossible à dire.

Des années et des années. Dizaines.
Centaines.
Après. Impossible de distinguer. L'entendu.
Signes. Paroles. Mémoire. Déjà
dit vient
de dire va
dire
Souvenir mal entendu, incertain.
La pluie rêve de sons. Des pauses.
Exhalation.
Des affirmations toutes les affirmations
en exhalation.

Peu à peu

Là, des années après, incertain si la pluie
la parole souvenues comment c'était comme
c'était comme si c'était.

Mordre la langue. Avaler. Profondément,
Plus profondément. Avaler. Plus encore.
J'usqu'a ce qu'il n'y aurait plus d'organe.

Images only. Alone. Images.
The signs in the rain I listened
the speaking no more than rain having become snow.
True or not
true
no longer possible to say.

Years and years. Ten upon ten.
One hundred upon one hundred.
hundreds   years   after. No longer possible
to distinguish.
The audible. Signs. Spoken. Memory.
Which was already
said to be
said just to
say will
say going to just say
memory not all heard, not certain.
Rain dreams the sounds. The pauses. Exhalation.
Affirmation all affirmations
in exhalation.

Little by little

There. Then. Years after. Uncertain if
the rain the speaking remembered how it had been
as it had been if it had been.

Bite the tongue. Between the teeth. Swallow
deep. Deeper. Swallow. Again, even more.
Until there would be no more organ.

Plus d'organe.
Cris.

Peu à peu. Les virgules. Les points.
Les pauses. Avant et après. Après avoir été.
Tout.
Avant avoir été.

Phrases silencieuses.
Paragraphes silencieux
des pages et des pages à peu près
en mouvement
lignes
après lignes
vider à gauche à droit.
Vider les mots.
Vider le silence.

No organ. Anymore.
Cries.

Bit by bit. Commas, periods, the
pauses. Before and after.
After having been. All.
Before having been.

Phrases   silent
Paragraphs   silent
Pages and pages a little nearer
to movement
line
after line
void to the left to the right.
Void the words.
Void the silence.

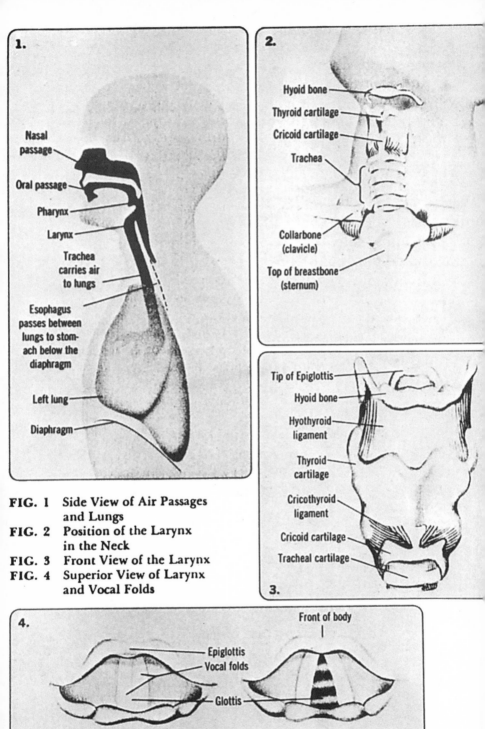

1. Nasal passage
Oral passage
Pharynx
Larynx
Trachea carries air to lungs
Esophagus passes between lungs to stomach below the diaphragm
Left lung
Diaphragm

2. Hyoid bone
Thyroid cartilage
Cricoid cartilage
Trachea
Collarbone (clavicle)
Top of breastbone (sternum)

3. Tip of Epiglottis
Hyoid bone
Hyothyroid ligament
Thyroid cartilage
Cricothyroid ligament
Cricoid cartilage
Tracheal cartilage

FIG. 1 Side View of Air Passages and Lungs
FIG. 2 Position of the Larynx in the Neck
FIG. 3 Front View of the Larynx
FIG. 4 Superior View of Larynx and Vocal Folds

4. Front of body
Epiglottis
Vocal folds
Glottis

a. Adduction of vocal folds for phonation

b. Abduction of vocal folds for breathing

One by one.
The sounds. The sounds that move at a time
stops. Starts again. Exceptions
stops and starts again
all but exceptions.
Stop. Start. Starts.
Contractions. Noise. Semblance of noise.
Broken speech. One to one. At a time.
Cracked tongue. Broken tongue.
Pidgeon. Semblance of speech.
Swallows. Inhales. Stutter. Starts. Stops before
starts.
About to. Then stops. Exhale
swallowed to a sudden arrest.
Rest. Without. Can do without rests. Improper
to rest before begun even. Probation of rest.
Without them all.
Stop start.
Where proper pauses were expected.
But no more.

MELPOMENE   TRAGEDY

produces by korean war

She could be seen sitting in the first few rows. She would be sitting in the first few rows. Closer the better. The more. Better to eliminate presences of others surrounding better view away from that which is left behind far away back behind more for closer view more and more face to face until nothing else sees only this view singular. All dim, gently, slowly until in the dark, the absolute darkness the shadows fade.

She is stretched out as far as the seat allows until her neck rests on the back of the seat. She pulls her coat just below her chin enveloped in one mass before the moving shades, flickering light through the empty window, length of the gardens the trees in perfect a symmetry.

The correct time beyond the windows the correct season the correct forecast. Beyond the empty the correct setting, immobile. Placid. Extreme stillness. Misplaces nothing. Nothing equivalent. Irreplaceable. Not before. Not after.

The submission is complete. Relinquishes even the vision to immobility. Abandons all protests to that which will appear to the sight. About to appear. Forecast. Break. Break, by all means. The illusion that the act of viewing is to make alteration of the visible. The expulsion is immediate. Not one second is lost to the replication of the totality. Total severance of the seen. Incision.

Dear Mother,

4. 19. Four Nineteen, April 19th, eighteen years
later. Nothing has changed, we are at a standstill. I
speak in another tongue now, a second tongue a
foreign tongue. All this time we have been away. But
nothing has changed. A stand still.

→ It is not 6. 25. Six twenty five. June 25th 1950. Not
today. Not this day. There are no bombs as you had
described them. They do not fall, their shiny brown
metallic backs like insects one by one after another.

*The population standing before North standing
before South for every bird that migrates North
for Spring and South for Winter becomes a
metaphor for the longing of return. Destination.
Homeland.*

No woman with child lifting sand bags barriers, all
during the night for the battles to come.

*There is no desination other than towards yet
another refuge from yet another war. Many
generations pass and many deceptions in the
sequence in the chronology towards the destination.*

You knew it would not be in vain. The thirty six
years of exile. Thirty six years multiplied by three
hundred and sixty five days. That one day your
country would be your own. This day did finally

come. The Japanese were defeated in the world war and were making their descent back to their country. As soon as you heard, you followed South. You carried not a single piece, not a photograph, nothing to evoke your memory, abandoned all to see your nation freed.

From another epic another history. From the missing narrative. From the multitude of narratives. Missing. From the chronicles. For another telling for other recitations.

Our destination is fixed on the perpetual motion of search. Fixed in its perpetual exile. Here at my return in eighteen years, the war is not ended. We fight the same war. We are inside the same struggle seeking the same destination. We are severed in Two by an abstract enemy an invisible enemy under the title of liberators who have conveniently named the severance, Civil War. Cold War. Stalemate.

I am in the same crowd, the same coup, the same revolt, nothing has changed. I am inside the demonstration I am locked inside the crowd and carried in its movement. The voices ring shout one voice then many voices they are waves they echo I am moving in the direction the only one direction with the voices the only direction. The other movement towards us it increases steadily their direction their only direction our mutual destination towards the other against the other. Move.

I feel the tightening of the crowd body to body

now the voices rising thicker I hear the break the single motion tearing the break left of me right of me the silence of the other direction advance before... They are breaking now, their sounds, not new, you have heard them, so familiar to you now could you ever forget them not in your dreams, the consequences of the sound the breaking. The air is made visible with smoke it grows spreads without control we are hidden inside the whiteness the greyness reduced to parts, reduced to separation. Inside an arm lifts above the head in deliberate gesture and disappears into the thick white from which slowly the legs of another bent at the knee hit the ground the entire body on its left side. The stinging, it slices the air it enters thus I lose direction the sky is a haze running the streets emptied I fell no one saw me I walk. Anywhere. In tears the air stagnant continues to sting I am crying the sky remnant the gas smoke absorbed the sky I am crying. The streets covered with chipped bricks and debris. Because. I see the frequent pairs of shoes thrown sometimes a single pair among the rocks they had carried. Because. I cry wail torn shirt lying I step among them. No trace of them. Except for the blood. Because. Step among them the blood that will not erase with the rain on the pavement that was walked upon like the stones where they fell had fallen. Because. Remain dark the stains not wash away. Because. I follow the crying crowd their voices among them their singing their voices unceasing the empty street.

There is no surrendering you are chosen to fail to
be martyred to shed blood to be set an example
one who has defied one who has chosen to defy
and was to be set an example to be martyred an
animal useless betrayer to the cause to the wel-
fare to peace to harmony to progress.

It is 1962 eighteen years ago same month same day
all over again. I am eleven years old. Running to the
front door, Mother, you are holding my older
brother pleading with him not to go out to the demonstration. You are threatening him, you are begging
to him. He has on his school uniform, as all the other
students representing their schools in the demonstration. You are pulling at him you stand before the
door. He argues with you he pushes you away. You
use all your force, all that you have. He is prepared
to join the student demonstration outside. You can
hear the gun shots. They are directed at anyone.

Coming home from school there are cries in all the
streets. The mounting of shouts from every direction
from the crowds arm in arm. The students. I saw
them, older than us, men and women held to each
other. They walk into the *others* who wait in *their*
uniforms. Their shouts reach a crescendo as they
approach nearer to the *other side.* Cries resisting cries
to move forward. Orders, permission to use force
against the students, have been dispatched. To be
caught and beaten with sticks, and for others, shot,
remassed, and carted off. They fall they bleed they
die. They are thrown into gas into the crowd to be

squelched. The police the soldiers anonymous they duplicate themselves, multiply in number invincible they execute their role. Further than their home further than their mother father their brother sister further than their children is the execution of their role their given identity further than their own line of blood.

You do not want to lose him, my brother, to be killed as the many others by now, already, you say you understand, you plead all the same they are killing any every one. You withstand his strength you call me to run to Uncle's house and call the tutor. Run. Run hard. Out the gate. Turn the corner. All down hill to reach Uncle's house. I know the two German shepherd dogs would be guarding one at each side, chained to their house they drag behind them barking. I must brave them, close my eyes and run between them. I call the tutor from the yard, above the sounds of the dogs barking. Several students look out of the windows. They are in hiding from the street, from their homes where they are being searched for. We run back to the house the tutor is ahead of me, when I enter the house the tutor is standing in front of him. You cannot go out he says you cannot join the D-e-m-o. *De. Mo.* A word, two sounds. Are you insane the tutor tells him they are killing any student in uniform. Anybody. What will you defend yourself with he asks. You, my brother, you protest your cause, you say you are willing to die. Dying is part of it. If it must be. He hits you. The tutor slaps you and your face turns red you stand silently against the door your head falls. My brother. You are all the rest all the others are you. You fell you died you gave your life. That day. It rained. It rained for several days. It rained more and more times. After it was all over. You were heard. Your victory mixed with rain falling from the sky for many days afterwards. I heard that the rain does not erase the blood fallen on the ground. I heard from the adults, the blood stains still. Year after year it rained. The stone pavement stained where you fell still remains dark.

Eighteen years pass. I am here for the first time in eighteen years, Mother. We left here in this memory still fresh, still new. I speak another tongue, a second tongue. This is how distant I am. From then. From that time. They take me back they have taken me back so precisely now exact to the hour to the day to the season in the smoke mist in the drizzle I turn the corner and there is no one. No one facing me. The street is rubble. I put my palm on my eyes to rub them, then I let them cry freely. Two school children with their book bags appear from nowhere with their arms around each other. Their white kerchief, their white shirt uniform, into a white residue of gas, crying.

I pass a second curve on the road. You soldiers appear in green. Always the green uniforms the patches of camouflage. Trees camouflage your green trucks you blend with nature the trees hide you you cannot be seen behind the guns no one sees you they have hidden you. You sit you recline on the earth next to the buses you wait hours days making visible your presence. Waiting for the false move that will conduct you to mobility to action. There is but one move, the only one and it will be false. It will be absolute. Their mistake. Your boredom waiting would not have been in vain. They will move they will have to move and you will move on them. Among them. You stand on your tanks your legs spread apart how many degrees exactly your hand on your rifle. Rifle to ground the same angle as your right leg. You wear a beret in the 90 degree sun there is no shade at the main gate you are fixed you cannot move you dare not move. You are your post you are your vow in nomine patris you work your post you are your nation defending your country from subversive infiltration from your own countrymen. Your skin scorched as dark as your uniform as you stand you don't hear. You hear nothing. You hear no one. You are hidden you see only the prey they do not see you they cannot. You who are hidden you who move in the crowds as you would in the trees you who move inside them you close your eyes to the piercing the breaking the flooding pools bath their shadow memory as they fade from you your own blood your own flesh as tides ebb, through you through and through.

You are this
close to this much
close to it.
Extend arms apart just so, that much. Open
the thumb and the index finger just so.

the thumb and the index finger just so.
That much
you want to kill the time that is oppression itself.
Time that delivers not. Not you, not from its
expanse, without dimension, defined not by its
limits. Airless, thin, not a thought rising even
that there are things to be forgotten. Effortless. It
should be effortless. Effort less ly
the closer it is the closer to it. Away and against
time ing. A step forward from back. Backing
out. Backing off. Off periphery extended. From
imaginary to bordering on division. At least
somewhere in numerals in relation to the
equator, at least all the maps have them at least
walls are built between them at least the militia
uniforms and guns are in abeyance of them.
Imaginary borders. Un imaginable boundaries.

Suffice more than that. SHE opposes Her.
SHE against her.
More than that. Refuses to become discard
decomposed oblivion.
From its memory dust escapes the particles still
material still respiration move. Dead air stagnant
water still exhales mist. Pure hazard igniting flaming
itself with the slightest of friction like firefly. The loss
that should burn. Not burn, illuminate. Illuminate by
losing. Lighten by loss.
Yet it loses not.
    Her name. First the whole name. Then syllable by
syllable counting each inside the mouth. Make them

rise they rise repeatedly without ever making visible lips never open to utter them.

Mere names only names without the image not *hers* *hers* alone not the whole of *her* and even the image would not be the entire

her fraction *her* invalid that inhabits that rise voluntarily like flint

pure hazard dead substance to fire.

Others anonymous *her* detachments take her place. Anonymous against *her*. Suffice that should be nation against nation suffice that should have been divided into two which once was whole. Suffice that should diminish human breaths only too quickly. Suffice Melpomene. Nation against nation multiplied nations against nations against themselves. Own. Repels her rejects her expels her from *her* own. Her own is, in, of, through, all others, *hers*. Her own who is offspring and mother, Demeter and Sibyl.

Violation of *her* by giving name to the betrayal, all possible names, interchangeable names, to remedy, to justify the violation. Of *her*. Own. Unbegotten. Name. Name only. Name without substance. The everlasting, Forever. Without end.

Deceptions all the while. No devils here. Nor gods. Labyrinth of deceptions. No enduring time. Self-devouring. Devouring itself. Perishing all the while. Insect that eats its own mate.

Suffice Melpomene, arrest the screen en-trance flickering hue from behind cast shadow silhouette from back not visible. Like ice. Metal. Glass. Mirror. Receives none admits none.

Arrest the machine that purports to employ democracy but rather causes the successive refraction of *her* none other than her own. Suffice Melpomene, to exorcize from this mouth the name the words the memory of severance through this act by this very act to utter one, *Her* once, Her to utter at once, *She* without the separate act of uttering.

ERATO   LOVE POETRY

saint Thérèse

She is entering now. Between the two white columns. White and stone. Abrasive to the touch. Abrasive. Worn. With the right hand she pulls the two doors, brass bars that open towards her.

The doors close behind her. She purchases the ticket, a blue one. She stands on line, and waits.

The time is 6:35 p.m. She turns her head exactly to the left. The long hand is on 6 and the short hand on 7. She hands her ticket to the usher and climbs three steps, into the room. The whiteness of the screen takes her back wards almost half a step. Then she proceeds again to the front. Near front. Close to the screen. She takes the fourth seat from the left. The utmost center of the room. She sees on her left the other woman, the same woman in her place as the day before.

She enters the screen from the left, before the titles fading in and fading out. The white subtitles on the black background continue across the bottom of the screen. The titles and names in black appear from the upper right hand corner, each letter moving down-wards on to the whiteness of the screen. She is drawn to the white, then the black. In the whiteness the shadows move across, dark shapes and dark light.

Columns. White. Stone. Abrasive and worn.

Whiteness of the screen. Takes her backwards.

Drawn to the white, then the black. The shadows moving across the whiteness, dark shapes and dark light.

Extreme Close Up shot of her face. Medium Long shot of two out of the five white columns from the street. She enters from the left side, and camera begins to pan on movement as she enters between the two columns, the camera stop at the door and she enters. Medium Close Up shot of her left side as she purchases the ticket her full figure from head to foot. Camera holds for a tenth of a second. The camera is now behind her, she is at the end of the queue. Long shot. Cut to Medium Close Up shot of her from the back. She turns her head sharply to her left. cut. The clock in Extreme Close Up. Same shot of her head turning back. She leaves the camera, other faces enter, of the others in line, and camera is stationary for a brief tenth of a second. Close Up shot of her feet from the back on the three steps leading into the theatre, camera following her from the back. She stops. Her left foot lifts back half a step then resumes. Camera is stationary, tilts upward and remains stationary. Pans to the right, while zooming out, the entire theatre in view. The theatre is empty, she is turning right into the aisle and moving forward. She selects a row near the front, fourth seat from the left and sits. Medium Close Up, directly from behind her head. She turns her head to the left, on her profile. Camera pans left, and remains still at the profile of another woman seated. Camera pans back to the right, she turns her head to the front. The screen fades to white.

Mouth moving. Incessant. Precise. Forms the words heard. Moves from the mouth to the ear. With the hand placed across on the other's lips moving, form-

One expects her to be beautiful. The title which carries her name is not one that would make her anonymous or plain. "The portrait of. . ." One seems to be able to see her. One imagines her, already. Already before the title. She is not seen right away. Her image, yet anonymous suspends in one's mind. With the music on the sound track you are prepared for her entrance. More and more. You are shown the house in which she lives, from the outside.

Then you, as a viewer and guest, enter the house. It is you who are entering to see her. Her portrait is seen through her things, that are hers. The arrangement of her house is spare, delicate, subtly accentuating,

ing the words. She forms the words with her mouth as the other utter across from her. She shapes her lips accordingly, gently she blows whos and whys and whats. On verra. O-n. Ver-rah. Verre. Ah. On verra-h. Si. S-i. She hears, we will see. If we will have to see if. If. We would wait. Wait to see, We would have to wait to see, Wait and see. If. For a second time. For another time. For the other overlapping time. Too fast. Slow your pace. Please. Slower, much slower. For me to follow. Doucement. Lentement. Softly and slowly. For a second time. For another time. Two times. Together. Twofold. Again. And again. Separately, together. Different place. Same times. Same day. Same Year. Delays, by hours. By night and day. At the same time. to the time. twice. At the same hour. Same time. All the same time. At the time. On time. Always. The time.

rather, the space, not the objects that fill the space. Her movements are already punctuated by the movement of the camera, her pace, her time, her rhythm. You move from the same distance as the visitor, with the same awe, same reticence, the same anticipation. Stationary on the light never still on her bath water, then slowly moving from room to room, through the same lean and open spaces. Her dress hangs on a door, the cloth is of a light background, revealing the surface with a landscape stained with the slightest of hue. Her portrait is not represented in a still photograph, nor in a painting. All along, you see her without actually seeing, actually having seen her. You do not see her yet. For the moment, you see only her traces.

"Letter of Invitation to the Wedding of Sister Thérèse of the Child Jesus and the Holy Face.

God Almighty, Creator of Heaven and Earth, Sovereign Ruler of the Universe, the Most Glorious Virgin Mary, Queen of the Heavenly Court, announce to you the Spiritual Espousal of Their August Son, Jesus, King of kings, and Lord of lords, with little Therese Martin, now Princess and Lady of His Kingdoms of the Holy Childhood and the Passion, assigned to her in dowry by her Divine Spouse, from which kindoms she holds her titles of nobility-of the Child Jesus and the Holy Face.

Monsieur Louis Martin, Proprietor and Master of the Domains of Suffering and Humiliation and Mme Martin, Princess and Lady of Honor of the Heavenly Court, wish to have you take part in the Marriage of

Until then. The others relay her story. She is married to her husband who is unfaithful to her. No reason is given. No reason is necessary except that he is a man. It is a given.

He is the husband, and she is the wife. He is the man. She is the wife. It is a given. He does as he is the man. She does as she is the woman, and the wife. Stands the distance between the husband and wife the distance of heaven and hell. The husband is seen. Entering the house shouting her name, calling her name. You find her for the first time as he enters the room calling her. You only hear him taunting and humiliating her. She kneels beside him, putting on his clothes for him. She takes her place. It is given. It is the night of her father's wake, she is in mourning.

their Daughter, Thérèse, with Jesus, the Word of God, the Second Person of the Adorable Trinity, who through the operation of the Holy Spirit was made Man and Son of Mary, Queen of Heaven.

Being unable to invite you to the Nuptial Blessing which was given on Mount Carmel, September 8, 1890, (the heavenly court alone was admitted), you are nevertheless asked to be present at the Return from the Wedding which will take place Tomorrow, the Day of Eternity, on which day Jesus, Son of God, will come on the Clouds of Heaven in the splendor of His Majesty, to judge the Living and the Dead.

The hour being as yet uncertain, you are invited to hold yourself in readiness and watch."

Her marriage to him, her husband. Her love for him, her husband, her duty to him, her husband.

Still the apprenticeship of the wife to her husband. He leaves the room. She falls to the floor, your eyes move to the garden where water is dripping into the stone well from the bark of a tree. And you need not see her cry.

She moves slowly. Her movements are made gradual, dull, made to extend from inside her, the woman, her, the wife, her walk weighted full to the ground. Stillness that follows when she closes the door. She cannot disturb the atmosphere. The space where she might sit. When she might. She moves in its pauses. She yields space and in her speech, the same. Hardly speaks. Hardly at all. The slowness of her speech when she does. Her tears her speech.

She climbs the steps slowly. While she climbs, the lake changes from the lake at dawn the lake at day the lake at dusk the lake at moonlight. The time passing over the lake. The time it takes her to climb the steps.

"I still cannot understand why women are so easily excommunicated in Italy, for every minute someone was saying: "Don't enter here! Don't enter there, you will be excommunicated!" Ah poor women, how they are misunderstood! And yet they love God in much larger numbers than men do and during the Passion of Our Lord, women had more courage than the apostles since they braved the insults of the soldiers and dared to dry the adorable Face of Jesus." He allows misunderstanding to be their lot on earth since, He chose it for Himself. In heaven, He will show that His thoughts are not men's thoughts, for then the last will be first."

Upon seeing her you know how it was for her. You know how it might have been. You recline, you lapse, you fall, you see before you what you have seen before. Repeated, without your even knowing it. It is you standing there. It is you waiting outside in the summer day. It is you waiting and knowing to wait. How to. Wait. It is you walking a few steps before the man who walks behind you. It is you in the silence through the pines, the hills, who walks exactly three steps behind her. It is you in the silence. His silence all around the unspoken the unheard, the apprenticeship to silence. Observed for so long and not ending. Not immediately. Not soon. Continuing. Contained. Muteness. Speech less ness.

It is you who know to hear it in the music so late in the night. Then it becomes you, the man, her companion, the live-in student accompanying her to school how many times as a young girl. It is you who hears his music for her while she sleeps. It is you sitting behind him looking at the moon the clouds the lake shimmering. You are she, she speaks you, you speak her, she cannot speak. She goes to the piano while he plays. You know that he cannot speak either. The muteness. The void muteness. Void after uttering. Of. Each phrase. Of each word. All but. Punctuation, pauses. Void after uttering of each phrase. Of each word. All but. Punctuations. Pauses.

They do not touch. It is not like that. The touching made so easy the space filled full with touch. The entire screen. To make the sequences move. In close up. To fabricate the response. So soon. Too

immediate. To make fully evident the object. The touch. Making void the reticence of space the inner residence of space. Not this one. It's not like that.

He plays the piano, his own composition as he would on the ancient string instrument. Abstract, but familiar to you. Ancient and familiar. You think you have seen this before. Somewhere else. In *Gertrude.* It is her, with her elbows on the piano. It is you seeing her suspended, in a white mist, in white layers of memory. In layers of forgetting, increasing the density of mist, the opaque light fading it to absence, the object of memory. You look through the window and the music fills and breaks the entire screen from somewhere. Else. From else where.

You know how it was. Same. For her. She would do the same. She would sit at the piano as her sadness grew in her breath without any destination. She would set before each note until the music would induce her and she would acquiesce.

From the other room you knew as she would begin playing. You walk inside the room, you sit behind her you knew the music, which ones.

Mother you who take the child from your back to your breast you who unbare your breast to the child her hunger is your own the child takes away your pain with her nourishment

Mother you you who take the husband from your back to your breast you who unbare your breast to the husband his hunger your own the husband takes away your pain with his nourishment

She asks if you want to sing a song and you move next to her on the bench and you sing for her as she plays for you.

Perhaps she loved him. Her husband. Perhaps after all she did. Perhaps in the beginning it was not this way. In the beginning it was different. Perhaps she loved him inspite of. Inspite of the arrangement that she was to be come his wife. A stranger. Stranger to her. The one that she should espouse. Decided for her. Now she would be long to him. Perhaps she learned to love him. Perhaps it was never a question. It was given. She took whatever he would give her because he gave her so little. She takes she took them without previous knowledge of how it was supposed to be how it is supposed to be. She deserved so little. Being wife. How it was. How it had been. Being

"I am only a child, powerless and weak, and yet it is my weakness that gives me the boldness of offering myself as *VICTIM of your love, O Jesus!* In times past, victims, pure and spotless, were the only ones accepted by the Strong and Powerful God. To satisfy Divine *Justice*, perfect victims were necessary, but the *Law of Love* has succeeded to the law of fear, and *Love* has chosen me as a holocaust, me, a weak and imperfect creature. Is not this choice worthy of *Love?* Yes, in order that I ove be fully satisfied, it is necessary that It lower itself, and that It lower Itself to nothingness and transform this nothingness into *fire.*

O Jesus, I know it, love is repaid by love alone, and so I searched and I found the way to solace my heart by giving you Love for Love."

woman. Never to question. Never to expect but the given. Only the given. She was his wife his possession she belonged to him her husband the man who claimed her and she could not refuse. Perhaps that was how it was. That was how it was then. Perhaps now.

It is the husband who touches. Not as husband. He touches her as he touches all the others. But he touches her with his rank. By his knowledge of his own rank. By the claim of his rank. Gratuity is her body her spirit. Her non-body her non-entity. His privilege possession his claim. Infallible is his ownership. Imbues with mockery at her refusal of him, but her very being that dares to name herself as if she possesses a will. Her own.

One morning. The next morning. It does not matter. So many mornings have passed this way. But this one. Especially. The white mist rising everywhere, constant gathering and dispersing. This is how it fills the screen.

Already there are folds remnant from the previous foldings now leaving a permanent mark. This cloth

She forgets. She tries to forget. For the moment. For the duration of these moments.

She opens the cloth again. White. Whitest of beige. In the whiteness, subtle hues outlining phoenix from below phoenix from above facing each other in the weave barely appearing. Disappearing into the whiteness.

once in certain mind to prepare a quilt now left unattended to some future time. Its purpose having been expended she opens it, spreads it again as if following a habitual gesture. She looks at it once more with a vague uneasiness as though she was missing a part to this very gesture that she could not remember.

It stings her inside. All sudden. Summons. Move. To simply move. Her body. Renounce no more the will inhabiting her. Complete. She changes her dress, shed to the ground, left as it fell.

She moves now. Quickly. You trace her steps just after, as soon as, she leaves the frame. She leaves them empty. You are following her. Inside the mist. Close. She is buried there. You lose her. It occurs to you, her name. Suddenly. Snow. The mist envelops her she appears from it. Far. On top of the hill. You have seen her there many times. The lake she has visited often. The lake behind her on her steps. The waiter comes out to greet her he says how early she is this morning she says she came to see the lake he says he will bring her tea. Everything is seen from above. Very far above. The two figures inside the mist mass shifting in constant motion. You are made to follow the waiter inside while he prepares tea made to wait with him and when you return with him you find her gone. The white table the two white chairs the waiter in his white jacket the mist thick and rising. Very far. Above. Again from above the waiter inside the large white corners running back and forth calling her name. Hardly visible. The corners.

"The smallest act of PURE LOVE is of more value to her than all other works together."

"Martyrdom was the dream of my youth and this dream has grown with me within Carmel's cloisters. But here again, I feel that my dream is a folly, for I cannot confine myself to desiring one kind of martyrdom. To satisfy me I need all. Like You, my Adorable Spouse, I would be scourged and crucified. I would die flayed like St. Bartholomew. I would be plunged into boiling oil like St. John; I would undergo all the tortures inflicted upon the martyrs. With St. Agnes and St. Cecilia, I would present my neck to the sword, and like Joan of Arc, my dear sister, I would whisper at the stake Your Name, O JESUS."

It had been snowing. During the while.
Interval. Recess. Pause.
It snowed. The name. The term. The noun.
It had snowed. The verb. The predicate. The act of.
Fell.
Luminescent substance more so in black night.
Inwardly luscent. More. So much so that its entry
closes the eyes
Interim. Briefly.
In the enclosed darkness memory is fugitive.
Of white. Mist offers to snow self
In the weightless slow all the time it takes long
ages precedes time pronounces it alone on its own
while. In the whiteness
no distinction her body invariable no dissonance
synonymous her body all the time de composes
eclipses to be come yours.

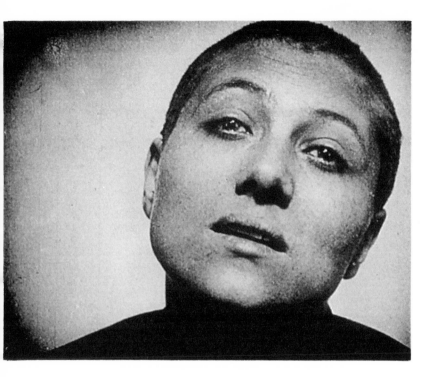

ELITERE LYRIC POETRY

korean idepcdence.

Dead time. Hollow depression interred   invalid to resurgence, resistant to memory. Waits. Apel. Apellation. Excavation. Let the one who is diseuse. Diseuse de bonne aventure. Let her call forth. Let her break open the spell cast upon time upon time again and again. With her voice, penetrate earth's floor, the walls of Tartaurus to circle and scratch the bowl's surface. Let the sound enter from without, the bowl's hollow its sleep. Until.

ALLER/RETOUR

Day recedes to darkness
Day seen through the veil of night
Translucent grey film cast between daylight and dark
dissolving sky to lavender
to mauve to white until night overcomes.
Hardly a murmur
Between dark and night
Suspend return of those who part with rooms
While shadows ascent   then equally fade
Suspension of the secret in abandoned rooms
Passing of secret unknown to those who part
Day receding to dark
Remove light   Re move sounds to far. To farther.
Absence full. Absence glow. Bowls. Left as they are.
Fruit as they are. Water in glass as beads rise to the rim.
Radiant in its immobility of silence.
As night re   veils the day.

Qu'est ce qu'on a vu
Cette vue qu'est ce qu'on a vu
enfin. Vu E. Cette vue. Qu'est ce que c'est enfin.
Enfin. Vu. Tout vu, finalement. Encore.
Immediat. Vu, tout. Tout ce temps.
Over and over. Again and again.
Vu et vidé. Vidé de vue.
Dedans dehors. Comme si c'était jamais.
Comme si c'est vu pour la première fois.
C'était. C'était le passé.
On est deçu. On était deçu la vue
du dehors du dedans vitrail. Opaque. Ne reflète
jamais. Conséquemment
en suivant la vue absente ↑
which had ceased to appear ↓ *translation*
already it has been
has been
has been without ever
occuring to itself that it should remember.
Sustain a view. Upon
itself. Recurring upon itself without
the knowledge of
its absent view.
The other side. Must have. Must be.
Must have been a side. Aside from
What has one seen
This view what has one viewed

Finally. View. This view. What is it finally.
Finally. Seen. All. Seen. Finally. Again.
Immediate. Seen. All. All the time.
Over and over. Again and again.
Seen and void. Void of view.
Inside outside. As if never.
As if it was seen for the first time.
It was. It was the past.
One is deceived. One was deceived of the view
outside inside stain glass. Opaque. Reflects
never. Consequently
following the absent view
which had ceased to appear
already it has been
has been.
Has been without ever

that. All aside. From then.
Point by point. Up to date. Updated.
The view.
Absent all the same. Hidden. Forbidden.
Either side of the view.
Side upon side. That which indicates the interior
and exterior.
Inside. Outside.
Glass. Drape. Lace. Curtain. Blinds. Gauze.
Veil. Voile. Voile de mariée. Voile de religieuse
Shade shelter shield shadow mist covert
screen screen door screen gate smoke screen
concealment eye shade eye shield opaque silk
gauze filter frost to void to drain to exhaust
to eviscerate to gut glazing stain glass glassy
vitrification.
what has one seen, this view
this which is seen housed thus
behind the veil. Behind the veil of secrecy. Under
the rose ala derobee beyond the veil
voce velata veiled voice under breath murmuration
render mute strike dumb voiceless tongueless

Discard. Every memory. Of.
Even before they could.
Surge themselves. Forgotten so, easily,
not even as associations,
signatures in passage. Pull by the very root, the very
possible vagueness they may evoke.
Colors faintly dust against your vision.
Erase them.
Make them again white. You Re dust.
You fade.
Even before they start to take hue
Until transparent
into the white they vanish
white where they might impress
a different hue. A shadow.
Touch into shadow slight then re turn a new
shape enter again into deeper shadow
becoming full in its mould.
Release the excess air, release the space between
the shape and the mould.
Now formless, no more a mould.
Make numb some vision some word some part
resembling part something else
pretend
not to see pretend not having seen the part.
That part the only part too clear was all of it was the
first to be seen but pretend
it wasn't. Nothing at all.
It seemed to resemble but it wasn't.

128

Start the next line. _→ order the reader._
Might have been. Wanted to see it
Might have been. Wanted to have seen it
to have it happen to have it happen before. All of it.
Unexpected and then there
all over. Each part. Every part. One at a time
one by one and missing none. Nothing.
Forgetting nothing
Leaving out nothing.
But pretend
go to the next line
Resurrect it all over again.
Bit by bit. Reconstructing step by step
step
within limits
enclosed absolutely shut
tight, black, without leaks.
Within those limits,
resurrect, as much as
possible, possibly could hold
possibly ever hold
a segment of it
segment by segment
segmented
sequence, narrative, variation
on make believe
secrete saliva the words
saliva secrete the words
secretion of words flow liquid form
salivate the words
give light. Fuel. Enflame.

Dimly, dimly at first
then increase just a little more
volume then a little more
take it take it no further, shut it
off. To the limit before too late before too soon
to be taken away.

Something all along a germ. All along anew,
sprouting hair of a root. Something
takes only one to start.
Say, say so.
and it would be the word. Induce it to speak to take
to take it
takes.

Secrete saliva the words
Saliva secrete the words
Secretion of words flow liquid form
Salivate the words.

*Dead gods. Forgotten. Obsolete. Past
Dust the exposed layer and reveal the
unfathomable
well beneath. Dead time. Dead gods. Sediment.
Turned stone. Let the one who is diseuse dust
breathe away the distance of the well. Let the one
who is diseuse again sit upon the stone nine days
and nine nights. Thus. Making stand again, Eleusis.*

RETOUR

→ return (handwritten annotation)

What of the partition. Fine grain sanded velvet wood and between the frames the pale sheet of paper. Dipped by hand over and over from the immobile water seemingly stagnant. By the swaying motion of two hands by two enter it back and forth the layers of film at the motion of a hundred strokes.

Stands the partition absorbing the light illuminating it then filtering it through. Caught in its light, you would be cast. Inside. Depending on the time. Of day. Darkness glows inside it. More as dusk comes. A single atmosphere breaks within it. Takes from this moment the details that call themselves the present. Breaking loose all associations, to the very memory, that had remained. The memory stain attaches itself and darkens on the pale formless sheet, a hole increasing its size larger and larger until it assimilates the boundaries and becomes itself formless. All memory. Occupies the entire.

Further and further inside, the certitude of absence. Elsewhere. Other than. Succession of occurrences before the partition. Away. A way for the brief unaccountable minutes in its clouding in its erasing of the present to yield and yield wholly to abandon without realizing even the depth of abandon.

You read you mouth the transformed object across from you in its new state, other than what it had been. The screen absorbs and filters the light dimming

dimming all the while without resistance at the obvious transformation before the very sight. The white turns. Transparent. Immaterial.

If words are to be uttered, they would be from behind the partition. Unaccountable is distance, time to transport from this present minute.

If words are to be sounded, impress through the partition in ever slight measure to the other side the other signature the other hearing the other speech the other grasp.

Ever since the whiteness.
It retains itself, white,
unsurpassing, absent of hue, absolute, utmost
pure, unattainably pure.
If within its white shadow-shroud, all stain should
vanish, all past all memory of having been cast,
left, through the absolution and power of
these words.
Covering. Draping. Clothing. Sheathe. Shroud.
Superimpose. Overlay. Screen.
Conceal. Ambush.
Disguise. Cache. Mask. Veil.
Obscure. Cloud. Shade. Eclipse. Covert.

Dead words. Dead tongue. From disuse. Buried in Time's memory. Unemployed. Unspoken. History. Past. Let the one who is diseuse, one who is mother who waits nine days and nine nights be found. Restore memory. Let the one who is diseuse, one who is daughter restore spring with her each appearance from beneath the earth.
The ink spills thickest before it runs dry before it stops writing at all.

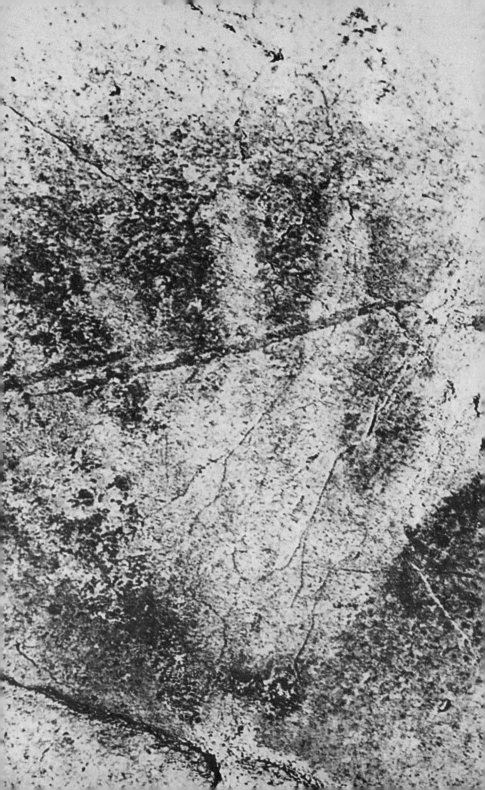

THALIA   COMEDY

She decides to take the call. Takes it at once. Her voice is as if she holds this receiver for the very first time. This foreign instrument that carries the very sounds to the words. The very words.

From when the call is announced to her to the moment she picks up the receiver she does not think. She hears the ringing and the call is announced. She walks to it, picks it up but she has not had the time to think. All had been prepared. All had been rehearsed beforehand. To the pause, over and over in her mind. The brief pause in the beginning before she would say yes. Each phrase according to its physical impact, its notable effect once pronounced to the accentuation of certain articles. To highlight the very objects that followed them. The voice would reach a crescendo, pause, begin again in a barely audible whisper with either coughing or choking at the throat. Rarely audible. Inaudible. Hardly audible at all. Reduced to a moan, a hum, staccato inhalation, and finally, a wail. She cannot contain any longer. Muffled through her door upstairs through another door.

She is the first to announce her arrival. Voice of anticipation. She wishes that it would metamorphose the other. The voice alone, by its force by its pleading by some inexplicable power. Of wishing. Wishing hard enough. She wishes that this person would be metamorphosed back into the person that was previously, she prays, invents, if it is necessary.

It took less time for her to realize that there would be no magical shifting. It did not matter anymore. She wanted to abolish it quickly, the formula, the ritual. All too quickly the form and the skin that resembles a past. Any past. With this, there would be no more rehearsals. No more memorization.

No end in sight. No ending and not a satisfactory one. One that might appease. If to appease was too much to ask for, then, sooth. Painless, at least numb. To keep the pain from translating itself into memory. She begins each time by charting every moment, the date, the time of day, the weather, a brief notation on the events that have occurred or that are to come. She begins each time with this ablution as if this act would release her from the very antiphony to follow. She begins the search the words of equivalence to that of her feeling. Or the absence of it. Synonym, simile, metaphor, byword, byname, ghostword, phantomnation. In documenting the map of her journey.

The extended journey, horizontal in form, in concept. From which a portion has been severed without the evidence of a mark even, except that now it was necessary to comply to the preface, "extension" to "journey."

There is no future, only the onslaught of time. Unaccountable, vacuous, amorphous time, towards which she is expected to move. Forward. Ahead. And somehow bypassing the present. The present redeeming itself through the grace of oblivion. How could she justify it. Without the visibility of the present.

She says to herself she could displace real time. She says to herself she could display it before and become its voyeur. She says to herself that death would never come, could not possibly. She knowing too that there was no displacing death, there was no overcoming without the actual dying.

She says to herself if she were able to write she could continue to live. Says to herself if she would write without ceasing. To herself if by writing she could abolish real time. She would live. If she could display it before her and become its voyeur.

Holyoke, Apr. 22, 1915.

Mrs. Laura Claxton,

53 Ashland Place, Brooklyn, N.Y.

Dear Madam:--

Noticing a postal card addressed to Mr. Reardon with your
name signed to same and having been living in the same apartment with hi
I thought I would let you know that Mr. Reardon has not been living he
since last July.

The last time I heard from him he was in Chicago, doing
and
Cabaret work as shortly after was taken sick.

Of late I have not heard anything from him and cannot advise
you of his present address.   I might also state that Mr. Reardon's
mother removed to Hartford about three months ago.

I shall keep your address in case I hear from him and will
pleased to advise you if you so desire.

Trusting this will be acceptable and hoping to hear from you
I remain,

Very sincerely,

H. J. Small,
173 Main St,

The line could be longer. Enough to observe the woman. One might say that she was crazy that in her eyes, either once doomed or more. Her pupils floating upward in the vast white. Her eyes fixed without a single blink on the profile next to hers, younger than a child more helpless than a child without the pride of a child even, they speak the truth of folly. Folly's truth. Her hand. Barely. Her forefinger. Barely climbs down from her hair to her lips. Her lips chafed by the cold. Parted slight. The forefinger touches the lip skin, as her eyes now close she might have sighed she might have moaned she takes the forefinger on her hand and barely reaches over to the shoulder the jacket where the pen is placed inside the pocket. She rests her finger there, just barely her mouth moves her eyes lift her smile her begging. If it was begging she might not have known it. The folly of innocence. The height turned away from her, against her, pays her no mind, is distracted takes his arm away. From her touch she must let go her hand clings to her chest where it's bare, unprotected from the layers of clothing, she moans inutterable language she cries the folly her pleading shame less in public take me open me take me now. The child. Less than child.

She is standing at the doorway. Now she is left to wait at the gate entry outside, the man has disappeared, she caresses the door she leans against the door as she would, her back against the day, the folly.

second memory

From under clothing. Cotton briefs stockings
brassiere slip over
progressively outward to external garments
adjoining days before appearances and finale
the bride of white three consecutive with each
appearance before the more white whiter marking
virginity in waiting to leap in a single day's time to
bride hood to wife once woman in waiting bride to be
at once
powder dusted skin scent upon scent the bathing the
dusting the layering of bottled perfumes gardenia
odorless gladiolas white chrysanthemums white
scents against white sheets to bleed upon
entwined cloth white heat white mist haze drizzle
own thickness white liquids to mingle foam retiring
against pulls prolonging the climax too long
prepared against the descent too soon to follow.
Virginity that misses
virginity consecrated. Already. Elsewhere.
It would not be unforgettable. It would be most
memorable. Of all. From any thing that is past to
any thing ever to follow. It would be reconciled
in this. Compensation for the absolute unattainable:
she memory of own birth and own death.
At the fulcrum. At which point in one's own time
flashbacks are possible and
anticipation.
Of the event that occurs once and only once.
Imagination harbors the desire of the object to

unlimited répétition at each point from the beginning to the middle to the end.
Rehearses the desire repeatedly, In preparation. Of the final performance.
Narrative shifts, discovers variation. Each observance prisoner of yet another observance, the illusion of variation hidden in yet another odor yet another shrouding, disguised, superimposed upon. Upon the nakedness. Nakedness as ordinary as common with all nakedness of all others before and all others to come. Like birth like death. Unlike birth, unlike death, *this* redeemed through a future and a past through own memory and presumes a separate conclusion.

Aug – 16 19,

Laura Clafton

Dear madam I
will write in regard
to your sister she
is an awful shape
she threatens
to Kill her self and
her children and
husband has done
all they can possibly
do and spend every
cent to dr. her they
can get and they
are haveing a time.
she is afraid of going
crazy. no dr can
do her any good she
has been to them a
and none do any good

at all but she wont
give up goes all the
time to them she
spends all the money
to dr. instead of to
get her something to
eat. and she is
afraid to eat. the Drs
say it will just
take time. all she
wants to do is ride
the roads and there
horses are all old and
wore out and very
near dead from hauling
her on the road
all the money you send
sure does help out they
are all broke and
dont know what to do

you wrote often to her
as your litters
cheer her up. She
has no fall hat
she said she would
get her something to
Eat with the you
sent her she likes
grape fruit & light
Bread that is about
all she will eat
          yours Truely
          a Friend

Memory

It is an empty theatre. The immediate familiarity upon entering the theatre, of that which has passed in shadow and darkness. It is between seances. The light from the street reflects on the screen briefly while the door opens and closes at a deliberate speed. The steps are carefully measured when darkness resumes, moving closer to the screen to the width of the screen, the depth.

She is the same. Sitting in the same seat four rows from the front and second seat from the left. It cannot be deciphered from her position and stillness whether she is waiting through the intermission from the previous seance or if she had just arrived. Her body is still. Her mouth slightly parted as before. Her eyes look ahead at no particular object or direction. She does not notice the presence of another person in the same row.

Second day in the theatre. Second time. She is sitting in the same place as the day before. As the first day. Turning left to see her, she is alone, immobile in her body. Her hands are folded on her lap with her other belongings. She hovers in a silent suspension of the simulated night as a flame that gives itself stillness and equally to wind as it rises. Her eyes open to distance as if to linger inside that which has passed in shadow and darkness.

She follows no progression in particular of the narrative but submits only to the timelessness created in her body. (Ancient. Refusing banishment. Refusing

149

to die, the already faded image. Its decay and dismemberment rendering more provocative the absence.) She remains for the effect induced in her, fulfilled in the losing of herself repeatedly to memory and simultaneously its opposition, the arrestation of memory in oblivion. (regardless. Over and over. Again. For the time. For the time being.)

Without a doubt she knows. She knows all along. How it is not easily believed. By her. By her even. Without a doubt she knows what she must say. All along. Even though. Not easily believed. Without a doubt the uncertainty of having said them bordering on regret without a doubt the wish to retreive them if she had regretted them afterwards all along. Now they retain their obligation as their own mass identity released to no individual being. Housed in their own. Scratch. Marking. Uncontainable. She knows during. While she says to herself she does not account for the sake of history. Simulated pasts resurrected in memoriam. She hears herself uttering again reuttering to re-vive. The forgotten. To survive the forgotten supercede the forgotten. From stone. Layers. Of stone upon stone her self stone between the layers, dormant. No more. She says to herself she would return time to itself. To time itself. To time before time. To the very first death. From all deaths. To the one death. One and only remaining. From which takes place annunciation. A second coming.

Before Heaven. Before birth and before that.
Heaven which in its ultimate unity includes earth

150

within itself. Heaven in its ultimate generosity includes within itself, Earth. Heaven which is not Heaven without Earth (inside itself).

Both times hollowing. Cavity. And germination. Both times. From death from sleep the appel. Both times appellant. Toward the movement. The movement itself. She returns to word. She returns to word, its silence. If only once. Once inside. Moving.

TERPSICHORE   CHORAL DANCE

極儀才象行合星卦連圍　環

太兩三四五六七八九重

1. 2. 3. 4. 5. 6. 7. 8. 9. 10.

You remain dismembered with the belief that magnolia blooms white even on seemingly dead branches and you wait. You remain apart from the congregation.

You wait when you think it is conceiving you wait it to seed you think you can see through the dark earth the beginning of a root, the air entering with the water being poured dark earth harbouring dark taken for granted the silence and the dark the conception seedling. Chaste the silence and the dark the conception seedling. Chaste you wait you are supposed to you are to wait for the silence to break you wait for the implanting of some dark silence same constant as a field distant and close at the same time all around sound far and near at the same time you shiver some place in between one of the dandelion seedling vague air shivering just before the entire flower to burst and scatter without designated time, even before its own realization of the act, no premonition not preparation. All of a sudden. All of a sudden without warning. No holding back, no retreat, no second thought forward. Backward. There and not there. Remass and disperse. Convene and scatter.

Does not move. Not a sound. None. No sound. Do not move.

Inside the atmosphere. No access is given to sight. Invisible and hueless. Even. Still. The thickness of the air weighs. Weight upon weight. Still. Heavy, inert is duration without the knowledge of its enduring.

Does not wait. No wait. It has not the knowledge of wait. Knows not how. How to.

Affords no penetration. Hence no depth, No disruption. Hence, no time. No wait. Hence, no distance.

156

Full.   Utter most full. Can contain no longer. Fore shadows the fullness. Still. Silence. Within moments of. The eclipse. Inside the eclipse. Both. Fulmination and concealment of light. Imminent crossing, face to face, moon before the sun pronounces. All. This. Time. To pronounce without prescribing purpose. It prescribes nothing. The time thought to have fixed, dead, reveals the very rate of the very movement. Velocity. Lentitude. Of its own larger time.

Withholds brilliance as the evanescent light of a dark pearl. Shone internally. As the light of the eclipse, both disparition. Both radiance. Mercurial light, nacrous. No matter, not the cloister of the shell. Luminous all the same. Waits the hour. To break. Then break.

For now, nothing enters. Still. No addition to the fullness. Grows, without accumulation. Augments, without increase. Abundance, Plenitude, Without gain.

Further, Further inside. Further than. To middle. Deeper. Without measure. Deeper than. Without means of measure. To core. In another tongue. Same word. Slight mutation of the same. Undefinable. Shift. Shift slightly. Into a different sound. The difference. How it discloses the air. Slight. Another word. Same. Parts of the same atmosphere. Deeper. Center. Without distance. No particular distance from center to periphery. Points of measure effaced. To begin there. There. In Media Res.

Do not move.
Not a sound. None. No sound.

Carrier, you hold in the palm of your hand the silver white spirit the lustre mass quiver and fall away from the center

one by one.
Sound.
Give up the sound.
Replace the sound.
With voice.

At a time. Stops. Returns to rest, again, in the center of your palm. You turn the seasons by the directions
South
North
West
East
Your palm a silver pool of liquid then as the seasons choose affix as stone in blue metal ice.

At times, starts again. Noise. Semblance of noise. Speech perhaps. Broken. One by one. At a time. Broken tongue. Pidgeon tongue. Semblance of speech.

You seek the night that you may render the air pure. Distillation extending breath to its utmost pure. Its first exhale at dawn to be collected. In the recesses of the leaves is an inlet of dew, clearest tears. You stow them before their fall by their own weight. You stand a column of white lustre, atoned with tears, restored in breath.

Maimed. Accident. Stutters. Almost a name.
Half a name. Almost a place. Starts. About to.
Then stops. Exhale swallowed to a sudden
arrest. Pauses. How vast this page. Stillness, the
page. Without. Can do without rests. Pause.
Without them. All. Stop start.

Earth is dark. Darker. Earth is a blue-black stone
upon which moisture settles evenly, flawlessly. Dust
the stone with a fine powder. Earth is dark, a blue-
black substance, moisture and dust rise in a mist. Veil
of dust smoke between sky and earth's boundaries. In
black darkness, pale, luminant band of haze. You induce the stone by offering exchange of your own.
Own flesh. Cry supplication wail resound song to the
god to barter you, your sight. For the lenience. Make
lenient, the immobility of sediment. Entreat with
prayer to the god his eloquence. To conduct to stone.
Thawing of the knotted flesh. Your speech as
ransom. You crumple and sift by each handful the
last enduring particle. Hands buried to earth dis-
solved to same dust. And you wait. Still. Having
bartered away your form, now you are formless.
Blind. Mute. Given to stillness to whiteness only too
still. Waiting. Scribe. Diving. In whiteness beyond
matter. Sight. Speech.

Cling. Cling more. At the sight of.
At last in sight at last. Cleared for the sighting.
So clear cling so fast cling fast at the site.
Clear and clearer.

Hours day sheet by sheet
one pile. Next pile. Then the next
from one pile to the next pile. One sheet below
the crack of closed door
slide piled up on the other side
no overlapping. One at a time. One sheet.
End in sight. With accumulation. Without prosper.

Earth is made porous. Earth heeds. Inward. Inception in darkness. In the blue-black body commences lument. Like firefly, a slow rhythmic relume to yet another and another opening.

The name. Half a name.
Past. Half passed.
Forgotten word leaving out a word
Letter. Letter by letter to the letter.

Open to the view. Come forth. Witness bound to no length no width no depth. Witness sees that which contains the witness in its view. Pale light cast inside the thin smoke, blowing. Then all around. No matter how sparse the emission, each subtle ascent is bared before the surrounding black screen. Then extinguish.

Emerge. Look forth. The succession of colors. Filtered beforehand to utmost. Pure. True. Stark. Foreboding. Red as never been. Bled to crimson. Trembling with its entire, the knowledge, of the given time. Given the mark of bloom, its duration. Abiding. Not more. Not less. The color that already was always was before its exhibition into sight.

160

Being broken. Speaking broken. Saying broken.
Talk broken. Say broken. Broken speech. Pidg-
on tongue. Broken word. Before speak. As being
said. As spoken. To be said. To say. Then speak

Immaterial now, and formless, having surrendered to dissolution limb by limb, all parts that compose a body. Liquid and marrow once swelled the muscle and bone, blood made freely the passages through innumerable entries, all give willingly to exile. From the introit, preparation is made for communion when the inhabitation should occur, of this body, by the other body, the larger body.

Stands now, an empty column of artery, of vein, fixed in stone. Void of wing. Void of hands, feet. It continues. This way. It should, with nothing to alter or break the fullness, nothing exterior to impose upon the plenitude of this void. It remains thus. For a time. Then without a visible mark of transition, it takes the identity of a duration. It stays. All chronology lost, indecipherable, the passage of time, until it is forgotten. Forgotten how it stays, how it endures.

A new sign of moisture appears in the barren column that had congealed to stone. Floods the stone from within, collects water as to a mere, layering first the very bottom.

From stone, A single stone. Column. Carved on
one stone, the labor of figures. The labor of
tongues. Inscribed to stone. The labor of voices.

Water inhabits the stone, conducts absorption of implantation from the exterior. In tones, the inscriptions resonate the atmosphere of the column, repeating over the same sounds, distinct words. Other melodies, whole, suspended between song and speech in still the silence.

Water on the surface of the stone captures the light in motion and appeals for entry. All is entreat to stir inside the mass weight of the stone.

Render voices to meet the weight of stone with weight of voices.

Muted colors appear from the transparency of the white and wash the stone's periphery, staining the hue-less stone.
wall.
For the next phase. Next to last. Before the last. Before completing. Draw from stains the pigment as it spills from within, with in each repetition, extract even darker, the stain, until it falls in a single stroke of color, crimson, red, as a flame caught in air for its sustenance.

Stone to pigment. Stone. Wall.
Page.
To stone, water, teinture, blood.

All rise. At once. One by one. Voices absorbed into the bowl of sound. Rise voices shifting upwards circling the bowl's hollow. In deep metal voice spiraling up wards to pools   no visible light lighter   no audible higher quicken shiver the air in pool's waves to raise all else where all memory all echo

POLYMNIA   SACRED POETRY

She remembered that she had once drank from this well. A young woman was dipping into the well all alone and filling two large jars that stood beside her. She remembered that she had walked very far. It had been a good distance to the village well. It was summer. The sun became brighter at an earlier hour, the temperature soaring quickly, almost at once.

Her mother had given her a white kerchief to wear on her head to avoid the strong rays and a lightly woven smock which was also white.

The heat rises from the earth, diminishing the clear delineations of the road. The dust haze lingers between earth and sky and forms an opaque screen. The landscape exists inside the screen. On the other side of it and beyond.

From a distance the figure outlines the movement, its economy, without extraneous motion from the well to the jar. The repetition of lowering the bucket into the well, an adept gesture that comes to her without a thought given to it, she performs it with precision and speed.

She too was wearing a white kerchief around her thick black hair braided in a single knot down to her back, which swung forward when she leaned against the well. She wore an apron over the skirt which she had gathered and tied to keep it from the water.

Approaching the well, the sound becomes audible. The wooden bucket hitting the sides echoes inside the well before it falls into the water. Earth is hollow. Beneath.

She did not look up at the young girl standing still before her. She saw her walking towards the well in slow paces, holding in her left hand, a small white bundle. Upon reaching the well she stopped still, no longer forced to pursue her pace. She opened her mouth as if to speak, then without a word, searched for a shaded area and sat down.

The proximity of the well seemed to cool her. She exhaled a long sigh. She closed her eyes briefly. The dust and heat had swelled inside them and she could not clearly focus her vision. When she opened her eyes, she could see the tiny pools of spilled water on the rocks surrounding the well and the light reflecting in them.

The second jar was almost full. She heard faintly the young girl uttering a sequence of words, and interspersed between them, equal duration of pauses. Her mouth is left open at the last word. She does not seem to realize that she had spoken.

She looked at the stone well, as the woman drew in the bucket. She followed each movement with her eyes. The woman rested the bucket on the rim of the well and reached inside her apron bringing out a small porcelain bowl. The chipped marks on it were stained with age, and there ran a vein towards the foot of the bowl where it was beginning to crack. She dipped the bowl into the bucket and filled it to the brim. She handed it to the child to drink.

She drinks quickly the liquid. Earth is cooler as it descends beneath. She looked up at the woman. Her eyes became clearer. She saw that the woman was smiling. Her brow fell softly into an arc on each side of her temples. Her eyes were dark and they seemed to glow from inside the darkness.

The child smiled back to her timidly from her seat. Her arms hugged her knees and her small palms wrapped perfectly the roundness of the bowl. The young woman asked her what she was doing so far away from home. The child answered simply that she was one her way home from the neighboring village to take back remedies for her mother who was very ill. She had been walking from daybreak and although she did not want to stop, she was very tired and thirsty, so she had come to the well.

The woman listened and when the child finished her story, she nodded and gently patted the child's head. She then brought over a basket and sat down beside her. The basket was filled with many pockets and she began to bring out one by one each pocket drawn with a black string. She said that these were special remedies for her mother and that she was to take them to her. She gave her instructions on how to prepare them.

She took off the kerchief that she wore and placed it on her lap. She took the bowl and said she must serve the medicines inside the bowl. After she had completed her instructions, she was to keep the tenth pocket and the bowl for herself as a gift from her. She placed the white bowl in the center of the white cloth. The light renders each whiteness irridescent, encircling the bowl a purple hue. She laid all the pockets inside the bowl, then, taking the two diagonal corners of the cloth, tied two knots at the center and made a small bundle.

She gives the bundle to the child to hold in her right hand and says for her to go home quickly, make no stops and remember all she had told her. The child thanks her and stands. She gives her a deep bow.

She began walking very rapidly. Her steps seemed to move lighter than before. After a while she turned around to wave to the young woman at the well. She had already left the well. She turned and looked in all directions but she was not anywhere to be seen. She remembered her words about stopping on her way and she started to run.

Already the sun was in the west and she saw her village coming into view. As she came nearer to the house she became aware of the weight of the bundles and the warmth in her palms where she had held them. Through the paper screen door, dusk had entered and the shadow of a small candle was flickering.

Tai-Chi	First, the universe.
Leung Yee	Second, Ying and Yang.
Sam Choy	Third, Heaven, Earth and Humans.
Say Cheung	Fourth, the Cardinals, North, South, East, West.
Ng Hang	Fifth, the five elements, Metal, Wood, Water, Fire, Earth.
Lok Hop	Sixth, Four cardinals and the Zenith and Nadir.
Chut Sing	Seventh, seven stars, the Big Dipper.
Bat Gwa	Eight, the Eight Diagrams.
Gow Gee Lin Wan	Ninth, Unending series of nines, or nine points linked together.
Chung Wai	Tenth, a circle within a circle, a a series of concentric circles.

Tenth, a circle within a circle, a series of concentric circles.

Words cast each by each to weather
avowed indisputably, to time.
If it should impress, make fossil trace of word,
residue of word, stand as a ruin stands,
simply, as mark
having relinquished itself to time to distance

Lift me up mom to the window the child looking above too high above her view the glass between some image a blur now darks and greys mere shadows lingering above her vision her head tilted back as far as it can go. Lift me up to the window the white frame and the glass between, early dusk or dawn when light is muted, lines yield to shades, houses cast shadow pools in the passing light. Brief. All briefly towards night. The ruelle is an endless path turning the corner behind the last house. Walls hives of stone by hand each by each harbor the gold and reflect the white of the rays. There is no one inside the pane and the glass between. Trees adhere to silence in attendance to the view to come. If to occur. In vigilence of lifting the immobile silence. Lift me to the window to the picture image unleash the ropes tied to weights of stones first the ropes then its scraping on wood to break stillness as the bells fall peal follow the sound of ropes holding weight scraping on wood to break stillness bells fall a peal to sky.

(handwritten annotations) → street · jiù/tenhòs · → Sacrea (linh thiêng). · → Sound that goes up · this poetry

179

Notes

1. F.A. McKenzie, *The Tragedy of Korea*, Yonsei University Press, Seoul, Korea pp. 46, 47, 236, 311, 312.

2. The Autobiography of St. Therese of Lisieux, *Story of a Soul*, A New Translation from the Original Manuscripts by John Clarke, O.C.D., ICS Publications Institute of Carmelite Studies, Washington, D.C. pp. 140, 168-69, 193, 195, 197.

Biographical material in CALLIOPE EPIC POETRY based on the journals of Hyung Soon Huo.

Calligraphy by Hyung Sang Cha.